POPULAR MUSIC

Cambridge Univ. Press { Division of ESQUIRE
510 N. Ave
New Rochelle NY 10801
Pop. Mu. in School - Vulliamy, Graham & Lee
8.95   ISBN 0-521-29727-3

Pop Rock & Ethnic Mu in Schools: " " "
9.50   ISBN 0-521-29927-6

Ord Transaction Books Bldg 4051
Rutgers St. Un New Brunswick
N.J. 08903
Whose Music? A Sociology of Mu. Lang.
7.95   ISBN 0-87855-818-2

Ord Metheun Books { Transworld Dist. Service Inc
80 northfield ave, Raritan center
Subculture; the Meaning of Style
6.95   ISBN 0-416-70860-9
Edison, NJ. 0881,

ROUTLEDGE POPULAR MUSIC

A series of books for schools edited by
Graham Vulliamy and Edward Lee

POPULAR MUSIC

A Teacher's Guide

Graham Vulliamy
Edward Lee

Routledge & Kegan Paul
London, Boston and Henley

First published in 1982
by Routledge & Kegan Paul Ltd
39 Store Street,
London WC1E 7DD,
9 Park Street,
Boston, Mass. 02108, USA and
Broadway House,
Newtown Road,
Henley-on-Thames,
Oxon RG9 1EN
Printed in Great Britain by
St Edmundsbury Press
Bury St Edmunds, Suffolk

Library of Congress Cataloging in Publication Data

Vulliamy, Graham.

Popular music.
(Routledge popular music series)
1. Music, Popular (Songs, etc.) - Instruction and
study. I. Lee, Edward. II. Title. III. Series.
ML3470.V84   780'.42'07   81-15683

ISBN 0-7100-0895-3   AACR2

CONTENTS

Preface to the Routledge Popular Music Series   vii

Acknowledgments   viii

Section I   Why this series?   1

Section II   Guidance for teachers and classroom
                 projects   13

        1   Introduction   15

        2   Alternative criteria: meaning and
             implications   17

        3   Rhythm in Afro-American music   26

        4   Singing   42

        5   Melody, harmony, counterpoint and
             form   50

        6   Orchestration, tone and timbre   56

        7   Popular song lyrics   63

        8   Youth culture   72

        9   Black studies   78

        10   References   87

Section III   Further resources   91

        11   'Folksong and Music Hall'
             by *Edward Lee*   94

        12   'Jazz and Blues'
             by *Graham Vulliamy*   98

        13   'Tin Pan Alley'
             by *John Shepherd*   103

        14   'Rock 'n' Roll'
             by *Dave Rogers*   107

        15   'Soul and Motown'
             by *Simon Frith*   111

16   'Reggae and Caribbean Music'
     by *Dick Hebdige*   114

17   'Contemporary Folk Song'
     by *Brian Carroll*   119

18   'Rock Music'
     by *Dave Rogers*   123

PREFACE TO THE ROUTLEDGE POPULAR MUSIC SERIES

Every teacher wishes to increase the motivation of his pupils.
Pop music is undoubtedly a major interest of many schoolchildren,
and there is no doubt that a growing number of music teachers,
having recognised this, are incorporating pop music into their
curricula. Those who have done so have found it entirely
compatible with the development of musicality, technical skill
and standards of excellence.

However, teachers who wish to use pop music need resources
and, hitherto, there has been nothing comparable to the many
excellent texts on aspects of serious music. This is the first
series of books about pop music designed specifically for school
use. Our aim has been to produce a text that is at once comprehensive and comprehensible, thus filling in the area that lies
between sophisticated texts produced for adults and the superficial products of commercialism. Accordingly, the texts have
been commissioned from acknowledged experts in the field, and
the series is edited by practising teachers who have demonstrated
their abilities as classroom teachers and in the field of educational
theory.

The 'Teacher's Guide' which accompanies the series is unique
in providing under one cover suggestions for classroom work, a
list of resources, and a compact summary of the essential theoretical background which a teacher requires to undertake a course
confidently.

ACKNOWLEDGMENTS

Many people have helped us with the production of this book.
However, there are some whom we would particularly like to single
out for thanks here. They are, first, all the contributors to the
series who have provided us with their contributions to section III
of this Teacher's Guide. In addition, we owe a special debt of
gratitude to both John Shepherd and Dick Hebdige: to John for
all the detailed help he has given us in clarifying our own think-
ing on the fundamentals of music and to Dick for allowing us to
plunder his profound knowledge and experience for the essay on
Black Studies.

We would also like to thank David Godwin of Routledge & Kegan
Paul for his advice and encouragement throughout the production
of this series, and Liz Hart and Jan Croall who did the picture
research on the pupils' books.

Finally, no acknowledgments could be complete without a
special thank you to our wives, Valerie Kilroy and Frances Lee,
for their unfailing support and continual good humour throughout
the duration of this project.

As editors, we have taken joint responsibility for the manuscript
and have therefore usually used the 'we' form in making points.
However, this masks a division of labour between the more sociological and the more musical sections of this book, which ought
to be specified. Thus Graham Vulliamy was responsible for section I
and the essays on Youth Culture and Black Studies (with Dick
Hebdige) in section II, and Edward Lee was responsible for all
the other essays in section II, with the exception of Alternative
Criteria which was jointly written.

SECTION I
Why this series?

WHY POPULAR MUSIC?

Traditionally, music education has concerned itself overwhelmingly
with 'classical' music. Yet a large part of the culture of young
people revolves around different types of 'pop' music. In an age
which is concerned to make education relevant to the needs and
interests of young people, it seems very strange that the
curriculum ignores almost totally the history and development
of popular music. This series of books serves to fill that gap
and to provide young people with an initial understanding of the
major influences on the music of their own culture.

   We believe that the appearance of this series will focus attention
on a divergence between the attitudes of the typical music teacher
and some of his colleagues, notably the teacher of social studies.
To the latter the relevance of such a series to the secondary
school curriculum will seem clear. Music cannot be divorced from
wider cultural and social issues, and nowhere is this relationship
more obvious than in the music of today's young people. Music
teachers, on the other hand, may find it more difficult to see any
justification for the series. Most will have received an intense
training in classical music. As a result, they may well believe
that a basic education in classical music will adequately equip
children to understand and evaluate any kind of music, be it
'serious' or 'popular'. The fundamental assumption on which their
belief rests is that there exists a set of 'absolute' and 'objective'
musical criteria in terms of which all music can ultimately be
judged, and which finds clearest expression in classical or
'serious' music. Often allied to this purely musical assumption is
the idea that classical music embodies the kind of ideal moral and
aesthetic values to which all young people should aspire. Yet,
paradoxically, both the musical criteria and the moral and
aesthetic values are seen as being essentially devoid of cultural
or social influences. Because of their obvious connections with
'mass society' and with commercial activity, on the other hand,
different types of popular music are seen as doing little but
debasing those values.

   Some recent publications have put forward a view of musical
value which contrasts strongly with that usually expressed in
music conservatories, university music departments and school
music departments. The book 'Whose Music?' (Shepherd et al.,
1980), for example, has argued strenuously that any particular
kind of music can only be legitimately understood and evaluated

in terms of the criteria of the group or society which makes and
appreciates that music. This principle may seem obvious to most
people. It has largely been accepted for many years by music
scholars in relation to most kinds of non-Western or 'primitive'
musics. Yet its implications have not been fully acknowledged
where the popular music of our own society is concerned.

This failure to accept such implications has had three important
consequences which are worth pursuing briefly here. First, there
has been little recognition of the view that the basic musical
criteria of traditional classical music and contemporary pop and
rock music are very different – a difference springing largely
from the development during this century of a new Afro-American
musical 'language'. Second, the concept of 'art' normally applied
to classical music is not appropriate to the discussion of pop
music, not least because pop, though a Western music, does not
aspire to meet Western 'art' criteria. Third, and partly as a
result of the first two consequences, pop music has not generally
been regarded as a suitable area for study in the music curriculum.

Different criteria

The importance of recognising the influence of Afro-American,
rather than traditional, musical criteria in contemporary pop and
rock music is argued in some detail by Vulliamy (1976). Because
different styles of pop music contain elements which, on the face
of it, are the same as those to be found in classical music,
classically trained musicians have in many cases been unable to
perceive the crucial differences that do in fact exist between the
two kinds of music.

Let us take an example to illustrate this. The twelve-bar blues
sequence, a simple structure based usually on only three chords,
has been widely used in various styles of popular music, from
New Orleans jazz to early rock 'n' roll to modern rock music. But
since much of the best classical music consists of lengthy pieces
with an elaborate harmonic structure, the twelve-bar structure
appears simple. The rock musician, however, sets out to work
within a harmonic framework like the twelve-bar blues. This
procedure has been likened to a chaconne, a comparison which is
somewhat misleading, since rock musicians use the structure
without varying it or manipulating it in any way that would be
greatly significant, in formal terms, to classical musicians. In
rock, the elaboration comes from inflections, notably of rhythm
and of the manner of approaching and articulating notes, and
from the importance placed on the highly personal timbres used
by individual singers and instrumentalists. Such an approach
derives from the fact that Afro-American music is an oral musical
tradition, involving the use of considerable improvisation, unlike
traditional classical music where the musical product is defined
by a notation system (see Wishart, 1980; and Greene, 1972).
Consequently, analysing popular music using the traditional system

of notation is very misleading. First, the blues or rock musician uses melodic effects (such as the bending of notes) and distortions of 'pure' tones, that cannot be accurately notated in a conventional manner. Second, the statement that a particular piece of popular music is in 4/4 (i.e. four beats to the bar) may make it appear simple rhythmically, but fails to indicate elements crucial to an evaluation of a piece, such as jazz 'swing' or a soul 'feel'.

It is therefore a central theme of this series that the criteria applicable to popular music are often very different from those applicable to classical music, and they need to be respected as such. Further elaboration of what these criteria mean and their implications for the classroom are dealt with in section II of this 'Teacher's Guide'.

Concepts of art

A second consequence of the failure to recognise the social context of music is an assumption that the standards used to judge classical music should be seen as the appropriate yardstick against which to judge all other contemporary music styles. However, the work of anthropologists, such as Merriam (1964), clearly demonstrates that such assumptions are misconceived. In our society classical music has, for various historical and socio-logical reasons, become an 'art object', increasingly divorced from the everyday lives of the majority of people. In contrast, popular music sets out to meet a wider range of social functions, including many which are traditionally seen by the Western art world as mundane and inferior. Once this is recognised, it becomes clear that criticisms of pop music made from such an 'artistic' perspective miss the point. We will illustrate this with two examples.

First, much pop music (particularly disco music) is condemned as merely 'dance' music in contrast to 'music for serious listening'. But to judge dance music by purely formal qualities such as are sought by the concertgoer is as serious an error as to judge a painting by a black and white photograph. Pop music has always been closely intertwined with dance and the outstanding pop musician has grasped the logic which makes for flow, making people want to move to the music. That this is an advanced skill can be demonstrated by comparing, say, the soul rhythm section of James Brown or the swing rhythm section of Count Basie with inferior imitators.

Second, much pop music is criticised for being commercial, a category which tends to reflect the assumption of a split between 'art' and 'entertainment' music. One of the best discussions of this issue is to be found in Pleasants (1969), who traces the origins of this split and challenges many of the assumptions embedded in it. With Pleasants we would stress that simply because a piece of music is either very popular or was produced

for commercial gain, it in no way automatically implies that the
result is musical inferiority.

Relevance to the school curriculum

The third and final consequence of the more traditional views
of music is that pop music has not usually been seen as a topic
fit for inclusion in the secondary school curriculum. There has
been a rigid distinction between what does, and what does not
count as school music. The majority of young people therefore
face a clear opposition between music which is acceptable to the
school, but which has little to do with their own culture or
interests, and the music of their own culture, which by inference
they are led to believe is of little value or significance. Such a
situation does little but exacerbate the conflict that already
exists in many areas between the cultural values transmitted
through schools and the cultural values of young people themselves.
   It is our belief, then, that the culturally relative view of music
which we are espousing here is not only a sounder one in musical
terms, but also has very beneficial pedagogical implications.
Further, it does not imply any rejection of a concern for standards.
There is no objective yardstick by which we can judge the relative
worth of, say, a great Louis Armstrong or even Jimi Hendrix
recording as against the recording of a Bach fugue since the
musical languages are in each case quite different. However, this
is not to say that we cannot make clear judgments relative to a
given set of criteria. If teachers' aims are 'the pursuit of
excellence', they can find it in any field, by applying their own
musical training and being sensitive to the variety of musical
languages used by different performers. The rock music of
Genesis, the reggae of Bob Marley or the mass pop of Abba are
all poles apart from each other in musical terms. Yet we can recognise
that, within their different musical genres, they are all masters
of their craft. To discover what musically separates such artists
from their many inferior imitators can only be a musically enrich-
ing experience for teachers and pupils alike.

CONTENT OF THE SERIES

Music teachers have at their disposal a large number of good
books designed specifically for secondary school pupils. However,
these books are restricted to music in the classical tradition
whether they are histories of music, biographies of the great
composers or descriptions of the instruments of the orchestra.
There has been no detailed, critical assessment of the history of
popular music designed for secondary school pupils. Instead the
latter have to rely on 'instant' biographies of the pop stars of
the day or on glossy books which aim to have a big short-term
impact, more by their range of photographs than by any serious

appraisal of the music itself. We believe that pupils deserve
educational texts on the music that makes such wide appeal to
them, texts which are as sound as those which deal with the
music that forms an important part of the European cultural
heritage. We hope that this series of eight books is a step in
that direction.

The books are: 'Folksong and Music Hall' (Edward Lee); 'Jazz
and Blues' (Graham Vulliamy); 'Tin Pan Alley' (John Shepherd);
'Rock 'n' Roll' (Dave Rogers); 'Soul and Motown' (Simon Frith);
'Reggae and Caribbean Music' (Dick Hebdige); 'Contemporary
Folk Song' (Brian Carroll); 'Rock Music' (Dave Rogers). Each
book discusses the major musical, historical and social developments within its particular area, as well as introducing some
key personalities and events.

The purpose of the first four books in the series is to provide
a historical background to the major influences on today's popular
music. Contemporary pop music embodies the fusion of two
musical cultures - the European and the Afro-American. The
story therefore begins with a survey of British popular music
prior to the Afro-American influence. Thus Edward Lee's 'Folksong and Music Hall' charts the major changes that took place in
British popular music before and during the nineteenth century.
The growth of industrialisation led to a decline in traditional
folk music and a corresponding increase in popular music designed
for a wider urban audience - a demand that was fulfilled in the
nineteenth century by the birth of the music hall.

Graham Vulliamy's 'Jazz and Blues' discusses the origins and
developments of Afro-American music. From the earliest slavery
days changes in black music have reflected changes in the
relationships of black people to white American society. A major
theme of the book is the enormous impact that black music has
had on contemporary pop music, as a direct influence on, for
example, rock 'n' roll, soul and rock. John Shepherd's 'Tin Pan
Alley' looks at the rise of the American commercial music market.
It was this tradition of song-writing that dominated popular music
throughout this century until the rise of rock 'n' roll in the mid-
1950s. Finally, in 'Rock 'n' Roll' Dave Rogers assesses the impact
of this musical form, showing in particular how it transformed
popular music into the expression of youth values that it has
remained ever since. Rock 'n roll was also the first music to make
essentially black music values internationally popular among white
youth.

The second group of four books in the series focus on more
contemporary styles. In 'Soul and Motown' Simon Frith looks at
the development of soul from its origins in the 1950s to the diverse,
commercially successful and influential music it is today. He shows
its impact on the rest of popular music - both directly, on musical
styles and conventions, and indirectly, through its popularity
with a white audience, particularly as disco dance music. Dick
Hebdige's 'Reggae and Caribbean Music' gives an account of the
emergence of Caribbean music, with particular reference to reggae

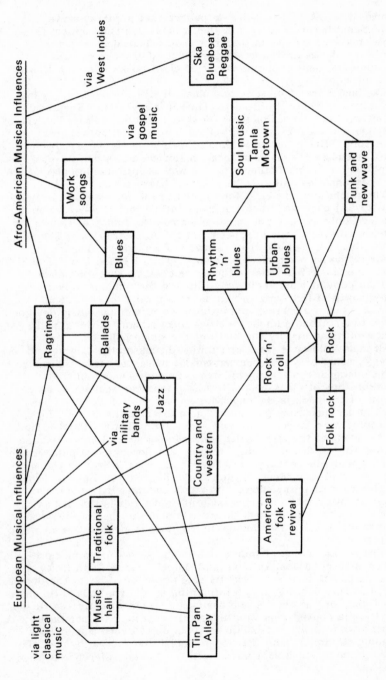

Diagram showing the interaction of European and Afro-American musical influences

and the related Jamaican styles, such as ska and rocksteady. Its importance in the British context derives from reggae's popularity not only with West Indian immigrants but with a large section of white youth as well. Key themes of this book include the religious and political connotations of reggae, notably its embodiment of Rastafarian beliefs, and the growing link between rock, white youth culture and reggae.

USING THE SERIES

The books have been designed as self-contained units, which hopefully will stimulate interest in the adolescent reader without any prior technical knowledge. They can clearly be used in a variety of ways. At one extreme the pupils' books, backed by this 'Teacher's Guide' could form the basis of a highly structured course on the development of popular music. At the other extreme, the various books could be dipped into by pupils for material on specific projects. Since our brief was to make them as informative as possible, in terms of personalities, facts, movements and dates, they could be used for reference purposes by pupils whose interest or academic training was insufficient to cope with excellent, but potentially daunting, works such as Gillett (1971).

The pupils' books are concerned as much with major social and historical themes as with strictly musical ones, reflecting our belief that music can only be fully understood in a social context. Consequently, they should provide new source materials through which teachers of social studies and integrated studies will be able to incorporate an important facet of young people's culture into the curriculum. We would also stress their possible use in history lessons, particularly, of course, social history, and English and drama teaching.

Music teachers will obviously stress the matters of more technical interest and each book is designed to provide an introduction to the key musical concepts of the field it covers. These concepts and any technical terms which are used are listed in the glossary at the end of each text.

Section II of this 'Teacher's Guide' gives, in compact form, a basic theoretical framework for approaching popular music as a social and musical phenomenon. We also suggest ways in which the ideas given may be turned into practical classroom activity. Finally, section III gives a list of further resources that may be useful in connection with the areas covered by each individual book in the series.

A NOTE ON DEFINITIONS

Our individual authors specify their own definitions of various musical styles in the different books. However, for the purpose of this guide we have assumed those definitions developed in the introduction to Vulliamy and Lee (1976):

Classical music is that part of the music in Western Europe from the Middle Ages to the present which forms the basis of conservatory training.

Afro-American is the term used for those styles of music which can be traced, in some of their aspects at least, to the merging of an African tradition of music with that tradition, European in origin, which thrived in the New World after the transportation of slaves. Examples of such styles might therefore include jazz, rock 'n' roll, blues, soul, Tamla Motown, reggae, rock music and the new wave.

Rock covers a vast area of music ranging from the more technically adventurous groups, whose music is to be found predominantly or even exclusively on LP records, to the more commercially orientated post-1964 derivations of earlier rock 'n' roll. It also covers the wide range of musical approaches thrown up by punk and the new wave.

Mass pop covers the wide range of styles (e.g. pop-rock, ballads, pop-disco) associated with the Top Ten singles.

Both rock and mass pop are influenced by Afro-American musical values to a greater or lesser extent; where the influence is strong and the music is actually played by black people the generic term 'black music' is often used. The term 'popular music' refers to the tastes of a substantial percentage or majority of the population. We reserve the term 'pop music' to delineate those areas of a popular music tradition which have been appropriated by young people in the post-1956 period.

It must be borne in mind, however, that these terms and their definitions are intended to provide no more than a basic frame of reference. In common with most classifications they are to some extent arbitrary.

FURTHER READING

Gillett, C. (1971), 'The Sound of the City', Sphere.

Greene, G.K. (1972), From Mistress to Master - The Origins of Polyphonic Music as a Visible Language, 'Visible Language', vol. 6.

Merriam, A. (1964), 'The Anthropology of Music', Northern University Press.

Pleasants, H. (1969), 'Serious Music and All That Jazz', Gollancz.

Shepherd, J., Virden, P., Vulliamy, G. and Wishart, T. (1980), 'Whose Music? A Sociology of Musical Languages', Transaction Books.

Vulliamy, G., and Lee, E. (eds)(1976), 'Pop Music in School', Cambridge University Press. New edition 1980.

Vulliamy, G., (1976), Definitions of Serious Music, in Vulliamy and Lee (eds), 1976.

Wishart, T. (1980), Musical Writing, Musical Speaking, in Shepherd
   et al., 1980.

SECTION II
Guidance for teachers and classroom projects

1 INTRODUCTION

This section of the 'Teacher's Guide' is devoted to a series of
essays which are designed both to explore key themes for the
guidance of teachers and to discuss various practical classroom
projects. The first, on Alternative Criteria, considers the implications for a teacher's classroom work of the view that popular
music needs to be approached and evaluated using different
musical concepts from those applied to serious music, and different notions of culture from those traditionally used in the assessment of art and high culture. The four essays which follow are
directed particularly at music teachers. They indicate what the
more general 'alternative criteria' thesis means in concrete terms,
with reference to key areas of our musical experience, and they
suggest a range of new classroom activities. The essay entitled
Popular Song Lyrics continues in similar vein but, because of its
subject-matter, should be of special relevance to English teachers
as well as to teachers of music.

We have directed the bulk of our teaching suggestions in
section II towards the guidance of music teachers. This is because
our experience suggests that many music teachers recognise the
need to incorporate popular music into their teaching, but lack
the knowledge to do so. The basic principles of oral-aural musical
traditions, like the Afro-American one, are very rarely dealt with
in the training of music teachers. Consequently, we see it as an
important role of a guide like this to fill in such gaps in the education of music teachers and suggest practical ways in which
popular music can be introduced into the classroom.

However, other subject areas have more readily incorporated
popular music into teaching. Chief among these have been the
teaching of social and general studies in schools and of liberal
studies in further education. Here teachers who are themselves
knowledgeable and enthusiastic about pop have used this medium
as a stimulus for both project work and the discussion of social
issues. Such teachers are rarely short of ideas. Nevertheless,
we thought it would be useful to end this section with some
suggestions of special relevance to such social studies teachers.
The essay entitled Youth Culture focuses upon one of the most
important sociological themes raised by any consideration of pop
music. The final essay, Black Studies, highlights the key role
that a study of contemporary popular music could play in an
important and growing area of the curriculum. It provides the
kind of detailed information which many teachers are acutely
conscious that they lack. Sound guidance is clearly of great

15

importance in an area of such social sensitivity.

These final two essays obviously by no means exhaust the potential use of this series in school subjects other than music. They should, however, be sufficient to act as a catalyst to enable other teachers to see the potential for project work from themes in the books of this series. Thus, for example, history teachers will find useful material on the effects of industrialisation and urbanisation in Edward Lee's 'Folk Song and Music Hall', and on the social effects of both war and depression in Graham Vulliamy's 'Jazz and Blues' and John Shepherd's 'Tin Pan Alley'. Geography teachers could use both 'Jazz and Blues' and Simon Frith's 'Soul and Motown' to highlight the causes and effects of black migration within the United States, and so on. This merely serves to demonstrate that any comprehensive survey of the origins, nature and impact of popular music in our society cannot help but be truly inter-disciplinary.

A NOTE ON REFERENCES

Since the various books in the series are referred to in all the essays, we have for convenience adopted the following abbreviations:

   'Folk Song and Music Hall' - (EL)
   'Jazz and Blues' - (GV)
   'Tin Pan Alley' - (JS)
   'Rock 'n' Roll' - (DR1)
   'Soul and Motown' - (SF)
   'Reggae and Caribbean Music' - (DH)
   'Contemporary Folk Song' - (BC)
   'Rock Music' - (DR2)

We have also listed all the references given in the essays in section II together at the end of the section.

2 ALTERNATIVE CRITERIA:
meaning and implications

It is sometimes argued that the use of popular music by teachers
constitutes an abandonment of educational and artistic principles.
We reject this view, since we believe that, apart from the value
of popular music as a means of motivating pupils, this field of
music, like all others, has its own intrinsic worth and system of
values. It is to this demonstrable network of values that we here
apply the term 'alternative criteria'. The purpose of the next few
pages is to indicate in more detail what the essentials of this value
system are, and in what ways it differs from received notions of
'culture'. We end by suggesting some of the implications of applying this alternative value system to school music teaching, with
especial reference to the use of this series.

VIEWS OF CULTURE

Before considering the term 'alternative criteria', it is useful to
clarify what people generally mean when they talk of 'culture'. In
particular one needs to understand the distinction that many
critics make between 'high culture', 'folk culture' and 'mass culture'.

A major concern of many discussions of culture has been the
possible effect of advanced industrialisation on the quality of the
artistic activities of a society. It has been argued that the standardised techniques of mass production and the intense commercialism of modern economies has led to a decline in the best of both
high and folk culture.

High culture is usually defined in terms of artefacts created by
a cultural elite within an established aesthetic tradition. It is
assumed that judgments are made of such products by critics who
are independent both of the producers and the 'consumers' of the
product, and hence have 'objective' standards. Folk culture is
usually defined as the traditional culture of people in rural en-
vironments, although since the evolution of industrialised urban
societies, some commentators have referred to an 'urban folk culture'. What is seen by many to be replacing traditional high and
folk culture is a mass culture, the term applied to the products
of a commercialised 'art industry', propagated through the mass
media.

Much cultural criticism during the twentieth century has centred
upon an attack on mass culture. Critiques have come from both
conservatives and from radicals - the literary criticism of F.R.

Leavis and T.S. Eliot being examples of the former, and the
writings of members of the Marxist Frankfurt School, notably
T.W. Adorno, being examples of the latter. The starting-point
for attacks on mass culture (in which popular music has often
been used as the principal target) is that such products are made
solely for commercial ends and that they are therefore necessarily
standardised in the interests of mass marketing. Consumers are
believed to be merely passive objects who are unscrupulously
manipulated and commercially exploited by the producers of mass
culture. In addition, the production of mass culture is assumed
to debase the quality of response to other cultural works, in that
it accustoms audiences to a version of the best high and folk culture in which depth, distinctiveness, and potentially disturbing
elements have been filtered out.

Whilst conservatives and radicals agree in many respects in
their criticisms of mass or popular culture, they disagree in their
explanation of the causes of the problem. Conservative critics
tend to emphasise the inadequacy of mass audiences, as the following quotations (Leavis, 1943; and Eliot, 1948 respectively)
illustrate:

> In any period it is upon a small minority that the discerning
> appreciation of art and literature depends; it is (apart from
> cases of the simple and familiar) only a few who are capable
> of unprompted first-hand judgement.

> It is an essential condition of the preservation of the quality of
> the culture of the minority, that it should continue to be a
> minority culture.

Radicals, on the other hand, blame not the audiences but those
who are alleged to regard cultural works as merely another form
of product to be sold in a mass market. Art (including music) is
thus as subject to the needs of business as any other product,
be it perfume or soap flakes. Art is necessarily debased by an exploitative process, which is concerned with the maximisation of
profits, rather than with the quality of the product or the best
interest of the audience.

We obviously do not share the negative judgments of such critics
of mass culture, at least in the case of music. We do not have
space to rehearse the arguments here, especially since many of
them can be found in Vulliamy (1976a) and Vulliamy (1980a). It
must suffice to say that the various assumptions underpinning
notions of high, folk and mass culture can be shown to be theor-
etically sterile and empirically invalid. In particular, analyses by
sociologists of the processes of legitimation of various art forms
show that such processes are highly culture-specific (see, for
example, Bourdieu, 1971). Even the 'highest' culture is not 'outside' or 'beyond' the influence of social and economic factors.

From our point of view, the greatest disadvantage of hostile
views of mass culture is that they are unnecessarily negative and

restrictive. Critics of popular culture usually do not recognise the
alternative criteria of quality specific to particular cultural products. Instead they misleadingly apply inappropriate critical canons
derived from analyses of high cultural works. In the case of popular music we argue for an alternative view, which is set out below.

THE CROSS-CULTURAL APPROACH

Perhaps the most important assumption which we make is that the
music teacher needs to view his subject in a less ethnocentric way.
We feel that a cross-cultural approach is the inevitable outcome
of an examination of world music in a spirit of rational enquiry.
Another result of such an examination is the recognition that the
study of other musical cultures can be aesthetically and education-
ally valuable to British schoolchildren - the practical need for
such an approach in a multicultural society should no longer need
stressing. The incorporation in this series of a book on reggae
(which is, at least in origin, a West Indian urban folk music) is
an indication of our commitment to the study of the music of other
ethnic groups as a part of a modern curriculum. Just as our view
of the nature of high cultural assumptions leads us to reject
generalised attacks on popular music, so our cross-cultural view
of music leads us to assert the value of Afro-American forms,
which constitute the bulk of modern popular taste. It should be
noted that the term 'Afro-American' is not merely a piece of academic jargon - the label reflects the way in which we interpret
the musical phenomenon, which contains elements as related and
yet as diverse as reggae and ballroom dance music. We should
mention, however, that some writers would prefer to distinguish
white derivatives (such as the music of Tin Pan Alley) from the
black traditions of the New World, to which they feel the term
'Afro-American' is more accurately applicable. We have preferred
to keep the term as a more general one, describing black music
by some such label, when necessary.

Because of the ubiquitousness of popular music through broad-
casting and recording, it is as familiar a part of our daily life
as the motor car or canned beans. We can therefore easily forget
that most of it is not a form of music indigenous to Europe, but
one which developed by 'acculturation'. This explains the paradox
that for some people (especially the young) the music is a per-
fectly natural phenomenon, needing no understanding; yet for
others (and especially classical musicians) the music is still largely
unknown, strange, or unacceptable. The difficulties of the latter
group are explained, at least in part, by the fact that popular
music tends to express itself through techniques alien to European
traditions since they originated in Africa. The popularity of the
music, particularly among older Europeans, tends to be in inverse
proportion to the use of 'African' elements.

From the foregoing remarks there follows a range of practical
implications, which we now list.

A cross-cultural syllabus

A possible scheme for a cross-cultural music course for the first
three years of secondary schooling is given below. It is stressed
that the examples are purely illustrative - many others could be
chosen. Moreover the basic structure is in no way prescriptive,
and is merely meant to initiate discussion among teachers as to
what might constitute a suitable balance. However, it should perhaps be mentioned that Farmer (1981) does point out some advantages of conceiving pop studies in terminal blocks. Nevertheless,
though we feel that our structure would be fully justifiable on
educational grounds, it is obvious that different teachers have
different personalities and in working situations may well feel a
need to reshape the structure fundamentally. We only wish to
assert: (a) that there should be a place at some point during a
pupil's general musical education for both popular and ethnic
music; and (b) that the study of such music can be a progressive
activity, leading to a development of the pupil's basic musical
concepts and skills.

Specimen syllabus:
Year one

Term 1	Popular music	From current pop (DR2) back to its roots (DR1). (Starts with pupils' interests.)
Term 2	Ethnic music	Africa to reggae (DH). (Development of 'Afro-American' theme; fosters good relations in multi-ethnic classes.)
Term 3	Classical music	'Avant-garde' music. On the lines of Self, Dennis etc.; links with primary school musical explorations; also with recent jazz (GV ch.6) and rock (DR2).)

Year two

Term 1	Popular music	Pop and jazz. (Attempt to generate technical interest; find new potential instrumentalists.)
Term 2	Classical music	Classical and Romantic music. (If necessary, starting from popularised versions of the use of classical themes and techniques in films and advertising.)
Term 3	Ethnic music	British and American folk music (EL,BC). (Encourage participa- tion; use of folk and rock material in rock and classical music; link up with history lessons.)

Year three*

Term 1	Social and economic back-ground	What the music means to us, what we use it for, what we expect of it – see Youth Culture, pp. 72-7.
Term 2	Technicalities of music	Appreciation of how it works – see pp. 25-62.
Term 3	History of music	Where it came from

*Syllabus dictated by personal interests because of the tendency of this age group to resist education.

Hopefully, interest will arise because pupils are able to choose a field which they have already found of interest, and because music is first approached as a social phenomenon (see Youth Culture). The 'project' approach would probably be especially suited to this work, with pupils following up their interests individually or in small groups. All the volumes in the series would be of use during this year, and could act as the basis of a resource file to be kept in the classroom or library, as appropriate. Naturally, some periods of teacher exposition and of discussion by the whole class are likely to be an important part of the course as well.

The following examples are meant to illustrate how pupils studying a particular field might use the books:

Rock 'n' roll	DR1, DR2 (development); GV (origins – especially chapters 7, 8).
Commercial pop	JS (origins), DR2. For accounts of use of suitable source material in the classroom see Burnett (1981) and Comer (1981a).
Classical music	Standard texts and histories, supplemented by EL (rise of classical music, influence on popular music), JS (acculturation), DR2 (meeting-points between rock and classical music).
Folk music	Nature and purpose (EL); American derivatives (BC).

Teachers seeking practical suggestions about the use of ethnic music in the classroom (including Caribbean and Indian forms) are referred to Vulliamy and Lee (1981).

INTEGRATED STUDIES

Another implication of our earlier remarks is that the understanding of music must be related to the purpose of usefulness of a music as defined by its audience. It is thus essential to see music in a social context, since different people encounter music in different contexts and with different preconceptions as to its nature.

This proposition is immediately applicable to the differences be-

tween popular and classical music. In particular, the popular
audience is more concerned with dancing, social participation, and
in some cases making music, than with attentive listening and
analysis. The teacher who understands and attempts to implement
these insights will find a need for some reassessment of his values
and some readjustment of his professional role. Possible roles for
the music teacher are discussed in Vulliamy and Lee (1976), and
an account of a successful change of approach towards pupils of
West Indian origin by a teacher of a previously 'traditional' orien-
tation is given by Spencer (1981b).

(1) Dancing: Popular music is very closely associated with
dancing; this is a fundamental point of divergence from the classical tradition. For expositions of the validity of music which is
combined with dancing and audience participation see Bebey (1975)
and Nketia (1975). Among the things which a music teacher can
do are:

    (i) organise dances and discos (or better still supervise
          organisation of such activities by the pupils themselves);
   (ii) organise lessons or a disco based on older styles. Pupils
          often have some interest in how young people danced in
          the past (e.g. the mid-1970s vogue for swing period music).
          Ideas can be found in EL, JS, DR1, SF;
  (iii) work with dance teachers to explore: existing dances; and
          movements created out of soul and similar music (see SF)
          to interpret the rhythmic structure of the music. Since
          the music often has three or four rhythmic layers (see
          Rhythm pp. 26-41, below) this can be a profitable
          approach to developing both dancing and attentive listen-
          ing.

The nature and role of dancing in popular culture is discussed
especially in EL, JS and SF.

(2) 'Rock musicals': A steady stream of these have been reported
in the educational press. They are frequently written by music
teachers themselves, though published materials do exist. But
pupils can also be very capable composers (see Vulliamy and Lee,
1976, especially chapters 5, 6, and 7) and should thus be encouraged. There is an excellent opportunity here for teachers of
music, English, drama, graphics and craft subjects to collaborate.

(3) Films: A large number of films of all periods feature popular
music; thus the British Film Institute (BFI) was able to mount a
four week season in 1978. Teachers should approach the BFI for
information as to what is available for hire at 127, Charing Cross
Road, WC2 (phone 01-437-4355). Any large bookshop will be able
to give the name of the various books which act as the encyclo-
pedias of films featuring jazz and popular music. Film hire can
be fairly costly, but can be justified to authorities on the grounds
that it is an aid which can often be used with all the classes in a
school.

The evolution of theatrical elements in popular music is discussed
in EL, JS and DR2. For earlier films JS (1920-40), GV (1940s) and

DR1 (1950s) would be valuable support or preparatory material.

(4) 'Graphic' project work: Especially with younger and less academic pupils, the collection and organisation of graphic materials is likely to be a profitable and welcome activity. Apart from the value to the pupils of taking decisions about the presentation of such materials, this type of activity is useful to the teacher who wishes to generate discussion, since there are a large number of starting-points in the collection of information about star performers, the examination of illustrated texts, and the collection of posters, musical journals, record sleeves and publicity photos. The teacher can ask questions, for example, about what can actually be seen (e.g. the star may well be in front of a backing group), what may be the 'content', purpose or implication of what is seen (e.g. in the above case the star and what he does are likely to be far more important in projecting to an audience than the music), the use of symbols (particularly clothing, hairstyles etc.), the use of colour (its impact), and in the art class, how the illustration is made (composition) and produced (techniques). These reflections seem perhaps to be too elementary to be worth a teacher's time. However, modern scholarship from a range of disciplines suggests that the way in which different people interpret the visual world is anything but simple, and that the questions are capable of an unlimited degree of sophistication. The use of visual symbols as a part of social interaction is an important feature of youth cultures (see pp. 72-7). The phenomenon is vividly brought to life by Dave Rogers and Dick Hebdige.

The above projects are clearly outside the field which many music teachers have been traditionally inclined or felt fitted to take on. We have already cited writings above, which seem to us to answer this argument. Experience shows that though the teacher is likely to start with insufficient expertise, this can be a situation which many teachers have found not only soluble but stimulating. (Arguments for pupil participation and that the teacher should not be an omniscient authority are given in Vulliamy and Lee, 1976; see especially pp. 49-61). Certainly with the type of work outlined above the pupils' motivation tends to increase, and a genuinely 'integrated' approach to follow easily and naturally.

Nevertheless, despite all that has been said above, we suspect that there will be few music teachers who do not continue to feel that their main purpose is to foster the performance, creation and appreciation of music, meaning by that word sound-structures which are conceived as separately existent entities, rather than as social symbols. 'Appreciation' will be taken to mean an activity involving intelligent reflection after attentive listening. To meet the needs of such teachers, we must examine the meaning of the phrase 'alternative criteria' still further, particularly with regard to the 'meaning' and techniques of music.

'MEANING' IN MUSIC

Except possibly in the case of some areas of modern serious music, most critics attempt to discuss music in terms of aesthetic and emotional effect. One regular line of argument against popular music, and especially against music produced primarily for intense commercial exploitation, is that the quality of emotion expressed is less worthwhile than that attributed to classical works. The question of what music means is one which is far too complex to be covered satisfactorily in this volume. Two examples of established viewpoints on problems of meaning in music can be found in Meyer (1956) and Cooke (1955). Cooke argues that melodic patterns can reflect fairly specific emotions. A critique of such established views from a sociological perspective can be found in Shepherd et al. (1980).

Once again, these 'theoretical' issues are not merely academic niceties. As in the matter of how music is presented through visual media, a range of questions can be discussed which will both develop insights into music, and increase pupils' skill in using words and presenting arguments. The type of discussion envisaged has the advantage of sidestepping some of the problems which can arise in the type of 'examination of issues' advocated by the Schools Council Humanities Project. The latter approach has had its successes, but can often fail to develop rationality because it deals with issues which are highly emotive to the pupil. We suggest that the juxtaposition of suitable recordings, supported by evidence from the texts, can be used to present phenomena which can be viewed as purely technical, but whose social and moral implications are open to development by the teacher if desired. To give a few examples:

TABLE 2.1

Topic	Problem/question	Source
Jazz/rock'n'roll	new, defiant, revolutionary or old, decadent, commercial	GV, DR1, DR2
Ragtime piano	a new art form (Joplin) or vulgar and commercial (classical view)	JS, ch. 3
Flat seventh	natural (folk view) or not musical (classical view)	EL

Other topics for which the books can act as a useful background, rather than as a specific source could be: black New Orleans jazz (earthy or crude? (GV)); rock drumming (simple and crude or exciting? (GV, DR1)); contemporary folk, rock (artistic (middle-class view) or feeble (view of punk and reggae fans) (BC, DR2, DH)).

TECHNICAL ASPECTS*

Whatever music may 'mean', it is indisputable that different cultures use different means of expression; for example, Northern Indian classical music uses no harmony. The main musical elements of Afro-American music are listed here briefly; an indication of further reading is given in brackets.

At the very centre of Afro-American music making lies an emphasis on rhythm. This subject is rarely discussed in any depth except in drumming manuals (but see also Jones, 1959; and Schuller, 1968; and DH). The other main medium of Afro-American musical expression is a personalised approach to tone and timbre (Hodeir, 1956; Vulliamy, 1976a). Systems of 'melody' making range from the European (Wilder, 1972) to an almost entirely African conception (Keil, 1966b; Titon, 1977; DH). Harmony basically follows European practice but with small but significant alterations according to style (Gutcheon, 1978; Harvey, 1975; Kerper, 1977; Lee, 1970; Sims, 1928). The method of analysis which is most appropriate to Afro-American music is still debated, but valuable insights are given by Chester (1970), Keil, Schuller and Titon. There is however general agreement that the effect and purpose of Afro-American forms are different from those of the classical tradition. We can note: evaluation of rhythm section (Keil 1966a; Lee, 1970); 'static' nature (Hodeir, 1956; Mellers, 1973); apparent monotony (Vulliamy, 1976a); 'folk' nature of pop (Belz, 1973); and nature and value of corporate composition (Lee, 1970; DR2).

---

*For further discussion see pp. 50-5.

3 RHYTHM IN
AFRO-AMERICAN MUSIC

GENERAL POINTS

All music, like all speech, has rhythm in some form. But the particular dimensions of rhythm which are exploited in Afro-American
music are one of the crucial ways in which Afro-American forms are
distinguished from the 'pure' European tradition. The historical
reasons for this have been discussed above.

Teachers need to bear in mind that there are many preconceptions about 'rhythmic' music which can hinder the appreciation of
Afro-American styles. Space does not permit the sort of discussion
which the topic merits, but we can note just two common assumptions, namely: (a) that 'rhythmic' (and especially percussive)
music is simpler than that played in symphony orchestras; and
(b) that 'rhythmic' (and especially dance) music is concerned
with a lower order of aesthetic experience. Both of these assumptions are extremely questionable, to say the least. Teachers are
thus asked to be on the lookout for the existence of such assumptions when preparing courses on the lines suggested below.

THE PRESENTATION OF RHYTHM

A system of analysis for approaching popular music is given below;
it is neither exhaustive nor prescriptive. This network of concepts
could be taught systematically, or it could be drawn upon during
the study of a given style or of the work of a particular artist.
It is assumed that teachers will both play and discuss records,
and engage the pupils in practical projects which will clarify,
reinforce and apply the understandings gained. This is the method
described by Comer (1981b).

Pulse

Attention should first be drawn to the fact that most music has a
pulse. Virtually any record chosen by the pupils is likely to mani-
fest pulse. However, valuable contrasts can be made with, for
example, the extensive use of rubato in some pieces of classical
music, the speech-based rhythms of some English folk music, some
twentieth-century 'classical' music, and some of the 'psychedelic'
pop of the 1960s. In these cases regularity of pulse is abandoned
with a variety of emotional effects, such as jaggedness, or floating

through space. Pupils can often respond adversely to music without a regular pulse. However, this need not be a disadvantage if
the teacher avoids head-on collisions over assertions of value, but
instead leads pupils to recognise and articulate that it is this
feature of the music which is unsatisfying to them. In so doing
they begin to map out their preferences in musical terms, and so
to understand basic musical concepts. Almost inevitably, pupils
will begin to see that emotional responses are elicited by musical
techniques. Such a recognition is central to the craft of much
music making, and especially that of an intensely commercial nature,
such as mass pop and film music. Examples of floating and evoca-
tive music abound in recordings of the late 1960s (DR2).

Tempo

The discovery that music can be classified as having or lacking
a pulse leads naturally to the consideration of tempo. The first
step should be to identify and clap the pulse of music of varying
tempi but with the same metre (the pupils are likely to be most
familiar and at ease with 4/4). The existence of tempo in a range
of musics which are otherwise contrasting can be demonstrated.
Jazz (especially bebop) provides excellent examples of extremes
of tempo. A startling comparison can be made between the frantic
tempi of much bop of the 1940s (GV) and British punk rock of the
1970s (DR2). Soul music (SF) and reggae (DH) are likely to produce some conflicting interpretations of tempo because of the pre-
dominance of cross rhythms and double tempo. Pupils can also
listen to music in which tempo alters (e.g. early blues), rallen-
tando (the endings of most small group jazz numbers of the 1950s),
and accelerando effects (e.g. Gary Glitter, 'My Gang'; the album
'Quo Live'). The attempt to clap out the pulse of very fast tempi
can provide some light relief provided that the teacher has a firm
control of the class. It is strongly urged that pupils should first
discover and execute pulse and tempo, in their own music, and
should only then be led to consider music which is less familiar
or less liked.
Italian terms indicating tempo should only be introduced after
the pupils have experienced and identified tempo. In the first
instance they should use English terms, including those of their
own invention (albums of popular songs produce some interesting
examples of unorthodox but effective terminology). Research in
linguistics suggests that technical terminology should arise in response to the observer's differentiation of experiences, and that
terminology which is effectively arbitrary (as Italian is to those
who do not speak it) is best introduced as a label for an insight
which has already been reached.

Metre

Pupils next need to grasp the meaning of this term. Though most
can find and follow a metre, as is evidenced by their ability to
perform dance patterns, they often find it difficult to pinpoint
the main accents consciously and to count them out. The existence and importance of metre can be demonstrated from any record
which has kept the 'count in'. (These appear from time to time,
especially in live recordings, and the teacher should look out for
appropriate examples.) The teacher can help pupils to identify
the first beat by drawing attention to recurrent features which
are associated with it in pop (e.g. bass and bass drum notes
often occur at this point). When pupils have gained this understanding from music such as country and western, which charac-
teristically emphasises the first beat, deviations from this pattern
can be shown, starting perhaps with the jazz 'break' (see p.
35, below) and going on to cross rhythms such as are found
in soul and reggae. One of the distinctive features of much
reggae is that the bass is given prominence; but instead of following out its most characteristic role of laying down the pulse,
it crosses the beat constantly (see Spencer, 1981b). Pupils familiar with this field are often very aware of this fact and can in
some cases execute examples of it.

Offbeat

One of the most important and distinctive features of Afro-
American music is that it emphasises the offbeat. This gives the
music a characteristic 'rocking' motion, as low-pitched notes on
the strong beats alternate with high-pitched (and hence pitch
accented) off beats. This phenomenon can be demonstrated first
from very clear examples such as can be found in country and
western and ragtime. Pupils can then be led to listen for the
stress given to the offbeat by the hi-hat cymbal in jazz. Any
solo by the drummer Art Blakey will illustrate his inclination to
keep this element of the structure when he has abandoned all
others. A clear exemplification of the sounding of the offbeat by
a pitched instrument (rhythm guitar) together with rimshot is to
be found in much rock'n'roll. The work of Philly Joe Jones with
Miles Davis illustrates the unusual procedure of using the rimshot
on the fourth beat only.
    The use of the offbeat can be traced through rhythm and
blues to rock, and also in soul, in which music it is often emphasised by high-register guitar chords. Finally the class should
look at the fairly small amount of more recent Afro-American
music which has rejected the emphasis of the offbeat in the
search for new rhythmic experiences. This can be seen in the
records of Miles Davis made at the end of the 1960s (GV) and in
the jazz rock of such groups as Weather Report. Such work may
lead on to African and Indian music, which also do not favour

a recurrent offbeat (see Cobbson, 1981; Floyd, 1981).

SUBDIVISION

Though subdivision of the basic pulse is a phenomenon which
occurs through classical music, Gunther Schuller (1968) has convincingly argued that Afro-American music exploits subdivision
in a unique way. Lee (1970) argues with examples that much of
the apparently loose feeling of some jazz solos is in fact an effect
of rapid interchange between subdivisions into two, three and
four. The pupils should thus become aware of the various types
of subdivision.
   (1) Subdivision into two: This is the predominant rhythmic subdivision of pop music after rock'n'roll. The latter style manifested
both the earlier swing and country styles (triplet subdivision)
and the newer blues and soul elements (duple subdivision).
   (2) Subdivision into three: Graham Vulliamy suggests that we
make comparisons between jazz and blues. This can usefully be
done with regard to rhythm. In particular blues music can be
analysed into those forms which use subdivision into two (typical
of rural and urban blues, and their rock derivatives) and those
which use a basic subdivision into three (e.g. the music of Leadbelly, Lonnie Johnson and Bessie Smith), a factor which faci-
litated links with and influence upon jazz, and later rock'n'roll.
The recognition of the triplet subdivision should be developed
in pupils, since it is so fundamental to style. To illustrate
the widespread use of triplet subdivision in music, examples of
appropriate classical music, Irish dance music, Tin Pan Alley
music, and recent 'funk' (SF) can be played.
can be played.
   (3) Subdivision into four: The phenomenon of doubling tempo
has been manifested in jazz since its early days, and examples
can be found in the work of Armstrong and his contemporaries
(GV). One or more instrumentalists may go into double tempo. As
might be expected, it is most commonly a characteristic of music
in a slow tempo, though some impressive examples of the doubling
of fast tempi can be heard in the recordings of Charlie Parker
(GV).
   In contrast, the doubling of tempo was at first uncommon in
pop and rock'n'roll. However, in the mid-1960s rock and soul
musicians slowed down the basic pulse of their music, and incorporated double tempo, giving a variety of rhythmic 'feels' (e.g.
'boogaloo', 'funky'). A similar phenomenon has recently been seen
in reggae, which also uses a fairly slow basic pulse (see DH;
Spencer, 1981a).
   Pupils should be encouraged to articulate their own experience
of such music. Once again, the labels they use should not be des-
pised, since they are often not merely fashionable jargon, but
reflect demonstrable differences of rhythmic configuration and
effect. Pupils should be asked to bring records to the class, and

to try to identify the sources of the 'feel', thus enhancing both attentive listening and stylistic discrimination. They should attempt to perform recurrent patterns, ideally on instruments, but certainly by clapping and tapping. Burnett (1981) shows how such work can lead easily and immediately to creative work by pupils.

The question of whether, say, a cymbal beat in semiquavers is an effect of double tempo or constitutes a fundamental element of rhythmic structure in the way that duple or triple subdivisions do is a matter which is possibly academic, and certainly cannot be discussed here. It is nevertheless vital to recognise that pop musicians regularly articulate such a rhythmic pattern and figurations based upon it. A discussion of the use of the semiquaver pattern in reggae is to be found in Spencer (1981b). The double tempo bass line is illustrated in Lee (1972); many further examples can be found in DeWitt (1976), Hammick (1975) and Kaye (1969-71).

The crucial point for pupils to grasp is that at least two things are happening rhythmically in such work. There is the articulation of a slow beat, and simultaneously one at twice the tempo. The musicians may work to one or switch between them. An important and basically new dimension of Afro-American rhythmic subdivision has been the use in funk, soul and jazz-rock of a basic pulse, subdivided into two (by the drummer and others). This subdivision (the double tempo) is then subdivided into three. This permits the rhythm section to create a typical rock 'feel', while the front line use typical jazz (triplet subdivision) phrases. The teacher will recognise in this procedure an excellent example of the phenomenon that the techniques and forms of a music reflect both artistic insights (into the possibilities of the form), audience response (a willingness to relate or accept relationships between two hitherto separate fields of music), and economic factors (front-line musicians with a jazz training needed new outlets for their skills as jazz declined in popularity). These types of interrelationship are an important part of the concept which underlies our series; we therefore recommend that teachers should try to find similar links in other areas of popular music and indeed of music as a whole.

SYNCOPATION, 'RHYTHMIC DISCORD', POLYRHYTHM, CROSS RHYTHM

It is indisputable that the characteristic rhythmic patterns of Afro-American music differ markedly from those of the classical music of the eighteenth and nineteenth centuries. Space precludes more detailed discussion, but the following points need to be made:

(a)   Much African music is polyrhythmic, i.e. it can be described in terms of rhythmic layers which are not derived from one basic metre.

(b)   There is undoubtedly some retention of African techniques

in Afro-American music, but individual lines are related
to a basic metre; yet they clearly do not reflect the stress
pattern of that metre as closely as does, say, the music
of Haydn. (The transformation of African rhythms is discussed in Schuller, 1968.)

(c) The analyst may fail to recognise his assumptions, and so
may be led to misinterpret what he sees; three terms which
need very careful handling in this respect are 'syncopation', 'resolution of rhythmic discord' and 'cross rhythm'.
(See also the article on Melody, pp. 50-1.)

(d) During the preparation of this text, John Shepherd argued
that we should first define syncopation as 'the displacement
of a rhythmic stress relative to a given metre.' We should
also note that syncopation commonly occurs in classical
music, but that it is a special effect.

(e) Shepherd then argued that to apply the term 'syncopation'
to Afro-American music is to transfer an inappropriate
term, since:

   (i) it is arguable whether the normal concept of 'metre'
   in classical works is an adequate description of the
   basic rhythmic patterns of Afro-American music
   (see (b));

   (ii) the term 'syncopation' implies an abnormal procedure, analogous to the process in earlier harmony
   of the creation of discords which have to be re-
   solved. It is because of the acceptance of this model
   that some writers are able to discuss the music in
   terms of 'the resolution of harmonic discords'.

(f) In contrast, Shepherd pointed out that what has often
been called 'syncopation' in Afro-American music is not a
special effect, but a permanently present structural feature
of the music.

(g) He further noted that the rhythmic patterns of Afro-
American music could be described in traditional terms as
'a series of syncopations'. This suggests that the patterns
consist of a series of separate stresses which are set against
a basic pattern (the metre). However, it seems likely that
what we have is a range of characteristic rhythmic patterns
which are superimposed over the basic pulse. These patterns might therefore more accurately be called 'cross
rhythms'.

Though further work needs to be done to test Shepherd's
hypothesis, we feel that his distinctions are worth making since,
as he has pointed out in discussion, it makes quite clear that we
are considering separate (even if interrelated) phenomena. The
terminology he advocates will then serve to remind us that the
role of Afro-American cross rhythm is not as a special effect to
'liven up' the music - it is a structural element. Further, we
should remember that the tendency of classical metres to dictate
the rhythm of all lines is a norm only for classical music, and not

for music of other cultures. Finally, we need to realise that there is no evolutionary development from the occasional classical syncopation through to 'advanced' Afro-American cross-rhythm, since the two musics come from different sources (we may be able, however, to suggest a development within Afro-American music towards longer and longer cross-rhythmic phrases).

Practically speaking, we suggest that the teacher should approach the development of a sense of accentuation which does not conform with the pulse from two directions. First, by taking typical examples of syncopation from the works of classical masters, and teaching them by imitation (as in Examples 1 and 2).

Example 1

Example 2

Second, by following out the type of scheme which follows, as an approach to Afro-American rhythm.

TEACHING AFRO-AMERICAN CROSS-RHYTHMS

It is suggested that pupils learn to hear patterns of the type indicated below. It is not necessary that they should be able to read them in notation in the first instance. Indeed, experience suggests that the difficulties of interpreting notation and of working out notated patterns according to the '1 and 2 and 3 and 4 and' system can stand in the way of the acquisition of these patterns, and can prevent pupils from realising that they are often already familiar with the patterns, can hear them, and can execute them.

It can be useful to begin the study of cross-rhythm by looking at 'anacrusis' ('lead in') which is a characteristic of much Afro-American music. Pupils soon learn to spot a drum or bass 'lead in'. Runs tend to begin off the beat (see Example 3).

Example 3

Such runs are also found in music with a triplet subdivision; hence Example 3(b) becomes Example 4.

Example 4

The advantages of an approach through anacrusis are (a) that it instils a clear sense of fixed points, and especially of the first beat of the bar onto which the above anacruses move; and (b) that the first note of each run is in fact the 'head' of a cross rhythmic pattern (see below). In much Afro-American music a basic quaver line is given a superimposed cross rhythmic accentuation (Example 5; see also, Lee, 1972).

Example 5

The teacher should then introduce in easy stages the crucial notion of emphasising notes which are between the main beats (see Example 6).

Example 6

It is usually helpful to the pupil to end up on a main beat, as in the examples given. One or more accented offbeat notes may be combined, culminating in an extended cross rhythm (see Example 7).

Example 7

Finally the teacher should introduce three patterns which pervade all styles. These are:

(a) The 2-4-2 pattern (Example 8):

Example 8

Here we have what is effectively a displaced bar, which can be filled and varied by inserting one of the cross rhythmic patterns already learned. Pupils familiar with the music described by Simon Frith will quickly come to recognise such patterns as being typical of bass parts in those idioms (Example 9).

Example 9

(b)   The 3-3-2 pattern (Example 10)

Example 10

This can be broken up into quavers (Example 11).

Example 11

It can also be used at half speed (Example 12).

Example 12

Any subdivision of the bars will work (Example 13).

Example 13

(c)   The 12/8 pattern: the 3-3-2 pattern can be subdivided
      so that one effectively has a 6/8 or 12/8 pattern (Example
      14).

Example 14

Most of the patterns given above are one-bar patterns. This is
a natural enough point to start at but pupils should be led as
soon as possible to deal with patterns of two, four and eight bars,
since these are more characteristic of the music. They should
come to see that all styles have a tendency to develop towards
more extended cross rhythmic patterns, a factor which may have
made them less accessible for those for whom the black American
tradition is not their 'native language'. For example, one could
compare the one and two-bar patterns of New Orleans jazz with
the longer periods of the bop musician. A similar development can
be traced from rock'n'roll through to 'advanced' groups such as
Grateful Dead and Weather Report.

SUSPENSION OF RHYTHMIC BASE

This type of technique is easily identified, but is none the less
highly effective. It is of great importance in Afro-American music,
and can take various forms:

1   A complete cessation of rhythm (the 'break'): such 'breaks'
    are counted out in strict tempo and last usually for two bars.
    The effect when the rhythm section resumes is electrifying.
    This technique is discussed in Spencer (1976a) and Lee (1972).
2   Out of tempo and rubato effects: this is a technique used
    mostly at the beginnings and ends of pieces. In the latter case
    it is a 'winding down' and was a stock feature of bebop. In
    the former, a slow, often reflective passage is played, before
    the group breaks into rhythm.
3   Change of rhythmic pattern: it is a common procedure in all
    styles to move from one type of basic rhythmic pattern to
    another. For example, a commonplace in the music of the
    1950s was a 'Latin' first section leading to a 'swing' main
    section. An early example of this approach is mentioned in
    JS ('St Louis Blues' moves between 'tango' and 'blues'
    rhythms). Typically, the group keeps a steady tempo, and
    similar rhythmic patterns but with a change of 'feel', some-
    times involving a doubling of tempo in one or more parts.
    Such changes are usually brought about by subtle but ident-
    ifiable changes in what the rhythm section does.

OTHER ASPECTS OF RHYTHMIC ARTICULATION

In presenting the technical elements of music the teacher will
naturally draw attention, among other things, to (a) 'expressive
techniques' and (b) questions of tone and timbre. These phenomena
are often seen largely as matters of 'colour' and 'feeling'. But
teachers should recognise that in Afro-American music at least,
such elements are inseparable from the creation of rhythmic
patterns. We therefore need to consider them now, since up to
this point 'rhythm' is an experience which has been defined
largely in terms of duration and accent.

One factor worth examination is the relation of pitch to rhythmic
expression, since pitch can be used in itself to give accentuation
to a note. Perhaps the most striking and widespread examples of
the use of pitch are in the articulation of the offbeat, as in the
use of the hi-hat (high pitch) on the offbeat, against the bass
drum (low pitch) on the onbeat. The rhythm guitar is also often
used to create a high-pitched offbeat sound, for example in
rock'n'roll and reggae.

Various factors traditionally associated with 'expression' are
used in Afro-American music as part of the rhythmic process. We
can note:

1   The use of 'pizzicato' and other forms of cutting short a
    note. Contrast the two bars of Example 15.

Example 15

2   'Slurring' notes. This effect is found in artists as diverse
    in conception as Coleman Hawkins (GV) and Jimi Hendrix
    (DR2). Those pupils who are interested in playing rock
    guitar can obtain a startling degree of sensitivity to this
    technique.
3   Timbre is an essential factor in the creation of both individual
    and group rhythm. Aspects which pupils can explore quite
    easily are the contrasts between electric and acoustic guitar;
    electric and acoustic bass; picked and plucked instruments.
    Picking and steel strings tend to generate more tension. A
    more 'swinging' rhythm is usually generated by acoustic
    instruments than by electric ones, possibly because the
    latter tend to sustain notes and are hence less percussive.
    Another useful contrast is between the jazz and rock drum
    sounds. The latter are normally tuned to a lower pitch and
    deadened by the use of masking tape on the skin and similar
    devices. Such practices account to a considerable degree
    for the different 'feel' created by the two types of group.
        Teachers should bear in mind that classical music tends

to reject personalised and discordant timbres. Against this
should be set the African scale of preferences, in which
harsh resonators may be added even to very 'mellifluous'
instruments such as the Kora (West African harp lute - for
further discussion see Bebey, 1975).

4   It should be realised that volume is a structural element in
much Afro-American music. It is not, when used by the
skilled musician, merely the result of a mindless insensitivity
to noise. Though the use of volume may well reflect responses to an increasingly noise-ridden environment, volume
is also used for purely technical reasons. High volume gives
a greater range of possible stress, and also alters timbre,
because different overtones predominate.

5   Articulation of the beat. A great deal of discussion has taken
place among writers on jazz about the placing of the notes
relative to the beat. In particular it is argued that 'swing'
in the jazz sense is at least in part caused by advancing the
beat slightly. For further discussion of this question see
Keil, 1966a; and Lee, 1972.

   A valuable exercise needing very attentive listening would
be for pupils to compare jazz, funk, reggae, rock'n'roll,
rock and commercial music from this point of view.

THE RHYTHM SECTION

It is characteristic of Afro-American music to have a rhythm
section. A record can thus be thought of as a 'total' rhythmic
statement. But it can also be seen as a creation in which a rhythm
section backs a soloist. Pupils should be asked to consider these
possibilities:

Do they feel that the rhythm section is merely a device for time-
keeping and marking the beat?

Is the music deficient when it lacks a rhythm section (e.g.
early blues, traditional English folk music, ragtime)?

What is the function of each player?

Pupils should be led to grasp the idea, which amateurs often find
difficult, that the notion of a rhythm section works against the
idea of individual expression, in which a complex effort by one
person grips our attention; to quote Spencer (1981b), for example,
'the criterion of reggae musicianship is the togetherness of the
group.' The rhythm section is a corporate activity in which complexity is subsidiary to accuracy and above all to appropriateness.
A rhythm section has its own set of values, which are in every
way as authoritative as those which we apply to the appreciation
of the European masters, but which differ in important respects.
Both musics stress the apparently universal musical principles of
shape or form, accuracy of performance, sensitivity to rhythm

and timbre, group co-operation, and the recognition of, and
sensitive response to, tradition. But the particular forms in which
these universal values are manifested vary considerably.

A major difference is that the term 'repetition' is defined and
evaluated in different ways. Both European and Afro-American
musics utilise repetition, without which a sense of pattern would
probably be impossible; the music would be an aural chaos. But
classical music exploits variations and transformations of rhythm,
linked with melodic patterning and harmonic progression to give
a sense of 'development'. Afro-American music prefers to exploit
the other possibility, the exact recurrence of shape. This leads
in some respects to a 'static' effect, but permits the musician to
explore the music in other ways. It is not mere 'liberalism' to
say that the two approaches cannot be judged against each other,
it is a matter of logic. In making any artistic work, the creator
has to make a series of choices, since he has to end up with one
product at any given point in time. He can thus, for example,
opt to repeat what he has just done, or to diverge in some ways;
clearly he cannot do both - the procedures are mutually exclusive.
(We recognise, of course, the vital element of repetition in a
classical recapitulation section, but this repetition occurs after
a phase of development, unlike Afro-American repetitions which
are frequently present throughout a piece.)

COURSE: THE RHYTHMIC SUBSTRUCTURE OF MUSIC

As a guide to teachers, and a summary of the above points, a
specimen course is outlined in Tables 3.1 and 3.2. For further
ideas on the teaching of Afro-American rhythm see Spencer (1976a;
1981b), Robins (1976) and Comer (1981b).

A certain amount of the work will be done by listening and discussion. But as far as possible the pupils should come to understand through doing. This is very possible, even with a large
class, since as Spencer (1976a) and Comer indicate, much can be
done simply by clapping and tapping. To this can be added any
percussion instruments that can be found or made.

The class can be organised in various ways. It can be treated
as a block; despite concern among some educational theorists
about this model, it has an honourable ancestry, and is the pattern
of much Afro-American music making (e.g. the preacher and
congregation). The class can also be split into competing or contrasting groups. This again is a time-honoured Afro-American
practice, as we can see from the big bands (JS, GV). For certain
types of work, the pupils can be split up into small groups which
work independently.

If suitable instruments are available, a rhythm section can be
formed, and can be used in the classroom (see Robins, 1976;
Lee, 1976b). Other pupils can comment, or can join in to play
other functions (sections, backing vocals). Notation can be used,
if desired, but teachers are reminded that an effective and usually

acceptable halfway house is that of using drummers' notation (see Lee, 1976a; Fisher, 1981).

TABLE 3.1

Term	Week	Topic	Comment/methods
One	1	Rhythm section (basic functions)	Listening, discussion
	2	Pulse	Clapping
	3	Tempo	Clapping, counting
	4	Metre	Clapping, counting, low-pitched percussion on main beats
	5	Offbeat	Clapping: introduce high pitched percussion; also contrast, say, feel of triangle and hi-hat
	6	Subdivision into two	Clapping, percussion, listening to examples; permutation
	7		of pairs of eight notes
	8	Subdivision into three	Same pattern: compare records built on duple and triple sub-
	9		division
	10–12	Recapitulation	Listening to and making music; with and without accented offbeat; and in duple and triple subdivision
Two	1–4	Syncopation	Approach from classical music, pupils make up own syncopated 'themes'
	5–8	Cross rhythms	Use of anacrusis: one and two bar cross rhythms
	9–12	Superimposed patterns	2-4-2 and 3-3-2*
Three	1	Breaks	Pupils invent 'fill-ins'
	2	Out of tempo effects	Mostly listening
	3	Pizzicato, slur	Small groups experiment with instruments, possibly taping their results
	4	Volume	Listening
	5	Timbre	Listening (the effective performance of rhythms with varied timbre tends to need a fair degree of skill)
	6–12	Rhythm section/percussion orchestra/combination with singers	Group activity, building up from and applying principles learned

Term	Week	Topic	Comment/methods
	10-12	Contrast of jazz and rock 'feels'	Listening

*In all the above pupils should learn patterns by imitation; this can be followed with a study of how the patterns are notated if desired. There should be much use of the call-and-response technique, with pupils improvising their own patterns. In the later stages percussion pieces could be worked out.

TABLE 3.2 A possible lesson outline: lesson 1, term one

Activity	Details	Comments
Play record		To illustrate rhythm section
Questions	What instruments? Tap out basic rhythm of each	Selective listening
Performance	Tap out what each is doing. Questions: Why do they do this? What happens if you do more, less, something different, at a different point?	Improvise different possibilities
Play record two	Rhythm section plus soloist or singer	
Questions	What do you notice first? Is the singer more important than the backing? Could he do without it?	Effect of removal of singer or backing – illustrate from dub or Gaelic records
	Would any rhythm section do?	Contrast rhythm sections of country and western, Hendrix
	What sorts of thing do they do?	Generate tension, fill in, create style?
	Is there any difference between featuring a singer and an instrumentalist?	Cream, Santana
	What if the focus is on a 'sound'?	Pink Floyd

The questions suggested in Table 3.2 clearly cannot exhaust the possibilities, and it is also obvious that answers would vary enormously in perceptiveness. Rather, our outline should be seen as the way a teacher would prepare in order to lead a guided discussion, moving on to activity. It would clearly be a very good lesson which only covered a fraction of the suggestions. But unless the teacher has foreseen some of the possible connections and developments he is unlikely to be able to make the best use of the responses of the class.

4 SINGING

Possibly no area of music is more likely to generate interest in
pupils and to result in creative work than pop singing. It is
equally probable that no area will cause the teacher more heart-
searching. There is first, as in the traditional singing class, the
problem of the adolescent's resistance to singing at a period of
recurrent social embarrassment heightened by problems of the
breaking voice. But more than this there are preconceptions and
prejudices not only in the pupils, but in the teacher himself.
Such feelings are intensified by the fact that in all music making
there is an element of social identification, of strong affinity with
modes of musical expression which act as symbols of the world-
view of the maker and of the audience (see Shepherd, 1980). It
is thus not surprising that lovers of classical music have charac-
teristically tended to see the pop singer - an untrained artist,
with a different, flamboyant appearance and 'exaggerated' mode
of presentation - as the epitome of all that is least to be desired
in music. It is perhaps salutary to remember that the stereotype
of the 'serious musician' in popular humour is likely to be a
gigantic Wagnerian soprano.

We argue that the stalemate of opposed viewpoints, which put
forward arguments that differ in verbal sophistication rather than
in quality of analysis, can be broken with musical integrity. Pop
singing, like all music, can be examined and defined in technical
terms. We feel that it would be valuable to adopt something like
the methods used by ethnomusicologists and linguistics scholars,
who set out to describe as 'scientifically' and accurately as possible
the sounds that they hear. From such descriptions it becomes
possible to construct a grammar of what is deemed to be acceptable
practice. It then becomes possible to make judgments about the
degree to which a given practice conforms to these criteria (which
are of course only applicable to the language or type of music
under discussion). In turn, those who wish to teach others can
use these findings in order to create suitable materials. Such
'grammars' exist for some areas of classical music (e.g. Andrews,
1958; Ulehla, 1966), but they need to be created for Afro-American
music, and in particular for singing.

POPULAR MUSIC OR POPULAR SONG?

The most superficial listening to the radio will indicate that popular
music is predominantly popular song. Instrumental backing is

universal, and instrumental interludes (solos, etc.) are common practice, but purely instrumental music probably does not account for more than two per cent of mass pop at the most.

The primacy of song, whether 'folk song' or 'popular song', is easily forgotten by instrumentalists both in classical music, jazz, and more recently rock. JS and GV, for example, write a great deal about the instrumental music of their field. But the core of the teacher's work is likely to be song, just as the core of DR1 is about rock'n'roll singers and rock'n'roll songs.

One should also beware of two common errors. One is that it is often believed that instrumental music, being more 'abstract', is thus a 'higher' form (Shepherd (1980) discusses this view, and examines it critically). A second error is the belief that skills achieved without formal training are inferior to those which require conscious study; thus pop singing is necessarily inferior to the classical forms. The fact that the untutored can acquire high skill in the use of their native language indicates the fallacy in this argument.

RELATIONSHIP TO AUDIENCE

At various points in EL attention is drawn to the fact that folk music is functional. This becomes self-evident if we think of work songs or lullabies. It is further pointed out that popular music is also functional, though in a somewhat different sense. It is used for dancing, and as an accompaniment to menial tasks. But it is presented in a different manner from classical music even when it is performed 'in concert' or on television (pop singers on TV usually have an audience). Without being pejorative, we suggest that it is generally true to say that the popular singer is an enter-tainer who projects to an audience, whereas the classical instru-mentalist is a performer who is observed by the audience. The classical singer lies between the two. But we suggest that he is more engrossed in the exquisite rendering of standardised work than with personal expression through the medium of music. He expects the quality of the score, brought out by his skill, to 'draw in' the audience to appreciation, whereas the popular singer is concerned with using a known system of techniques to manipu-late and 'draw out' the audience's own inner feelings - he goes out to get them to come across to him.

If the above is correct, then differences in teaching strategy are implied. Singing (like all creative work) must be drawn from the pupils and not imposed. It must be meaningful to them, and be deemed to be so by their peers or potential audience. The audience cannot automatically be dismissed. As a consequence extracurricular work, especially in the form of public performances, seems to be indicated. Such work needs to be seen as an essential part of the teaching process, not as an ancillary 'to keep the kids off the streets'. The effectiveness of such a redefinition of the role of the music teacher is described in Nicholls (1976) and

Vulliamy (1976b). This requires, however, that greater recognition is given to the fact that music teachers, unlike other teachers, undertake extracurricular work as a *necessary* part of their teaching load.

RELATION OF WORDS TO MELODY LINE

This topic is at the very centre of any training in singing. Thus one cannot hope to do it justice in the space available. We therefore present the following observations, accepting that they must necessarily be overgeneralised in some respects:

1 It is fallacious to assume that the lyrics of popular songs are meaningless or meant to be so (see BC).
2 There is a strong tendency for classical singing to be conceived in instrumental terms, as part of an instrumental texture, and for training in singing to follow an instrumental model (scales etc).
3 To some degree this tends to 'smooth out' any tendency to a speech-like delivery in favour of an instrumental criterion of good (even and controlled) tone. No judgment is implied by this statement. All singers have to strike a balance between the demands of words as pure units of speech and the demands of notes as pure music.
4 Under the influence of the black Afro-American tradition and of popular concepts of lyrics and of singing, popular singing has tended towards a dramatic, speech-like delivery. This can be seen in extreme form in recent new wave work. It can be contrasted to the straight delivery of tune in dance bands of the interwar period. JS describes the move away from this concept in some detail.
5 As a result of the above, the teacher should to some extent move away from the aim of instilling a standard conservatory tone or some acceptable modification of it, towards drawing out an interpretation from a consideration of the words. This approach is common practice in the training of actors, who have to learn to 'project', but who may be poor singers in a conventional sense. Links with English and drama teachers might be helpful in this respect. Lessons should mix both performances by pupils with attentive listening to and consideration of the technique of earlier artists.
6 We recognise that weighty arguments about the formation of vocal habits can be put forward. These are discussed - together with the problem of habit formation in general - in Lee (1981a and 1981b).

THE BLACK TRADITION

JS and GV both trace the influence of the black American tradition upon popular singers of all styles. The point is reinforced by the account of the development of Elvis Presley (DR1). DH presents another way of looking at the Afro-American tradition. Further ideas which will enhance understanding of this crucial influence in popular music are to be found in Vulliamy and Lee (1976; 1981). The points the teacher needs to understand are:

1 The basic outline of the black tradition (GV), the nature of its techniques, and its transformation into jazz and rock.
2 What constitutes a good usage of 'blues' techniques: Ideally a teacher would be able to use them himself, but the most important thing is to be able to recognise qualities in others which are not one's own (Spencer, 1976a).
3 That such techniques are not readily susceptible to notation: They need to be acquired orally, by face-to-face teaching, by the imitation of recordings, or of cassettes prepared on the lines of a language laboratory course.
4 That black American music is a tradition: In the first instance it will thus require imitation rather than innovation. Only after a period of imitation of works performed according to accepted - even if not explicitly stated - rules, can the pupil internalise such rules well enough to be able to recognise what are legitimate innovations. Work in a tradition such as the blues is undoubtedly creative, but it is so within very definite limits. This is in marked contrast to modern 'avant garde' approaches which seek to encourage a form of creative exploration which subjects the basic materials of music to much more radical reworking.
5 That the black tradition is 'intensional' (using the terminology of Chester, 1970): This means that the music has to be evaluated on grounds of skill and effectiveness in using the expressive devices of the idiom, and not by European criteria of 'tunefulness' or 'extended form'.

In order to advance pupils' understanding of this tradition we again recommend a mixture of close listening and creative work. The latter can be staggeringly good (see Spencer, 1976b). It is worth remembering that pupils of Caribbean origin may feel happier about approaching these matters through reggae than through music of North American origin. When one first becomes aware of the existence of a tradition derived from Africa, it is easy to lump together as 'black music' forms which are in fact perceived as highly disparate by their audiences.

INDIVIDUALISED TONE AND ENSEMBLE WORK

The search by Afro-American musicians for a personal tone has
already been mentioned and need be discussed no further. From
the teacher's viewpoint we note: (1) that pupils should be
encouraged to differentiate and ideally to articulate in words the
qualities of different tones; and (2) that the individualism of
popular music presents potential but not inevitable difficulties
of classroom organisation for teachers.

It might at first sight seem that, if the emphasis in popular
singing is on the individual, work must therefore take an individualised path of the sort described in Spencer (1976b) and
Nicholls (1976). We agree that this is desirable, since it breaks
the pattern of earlier teaching in which singing was seen predominantly as a choral activity; the individual is encouraged to
express himself.

The gains of such an approach can be very great since, as
Spencer (1976b), describes, young pop singers are capable of
responding quickly to positive criticism and to new influences,
and of making very marked advances in skill and conception.
Apart from making available his reservoir of technical knowledge,
the teacher's role (and here the series can be of great help) is
to point out that all artists have influences. Many look back to
earlier idols whom they learn to imitate before maturing into their
own individual style. For example, Billie Holliday and Judy Garland
have influenced a huge number of singers. Similarly, the influence
of Bob Dylan on a whole generation of singers is charted by BC.
The question of influence and innovation is a major theme in JS,
whose remarks on Al Jolson and Bing Crosby should be read.
Other important examples of influence which can be cited and
whose recordings should be compared are Ray Charles and Joe
Cocker (SF); Sam Cooke and Rod Stewart (SF); and Johnny Ray,
Mick Jagger and Rod Stewart (JS). One should also not forget
that some singers have chosen to draw inspiration from instrumentalists. JS details this with regard to Frank Sinatra, and Lee
(1970) describes how Bing Crosby learned from jazz records. The
imitation of instrumental techniques is a further minor, but valued,
strand of the popular singing tradition; one can quote the work
of Ella Fitzgerald, Cleo Laine, King Pleasure (in the 1950s), and
more recently the influence of (among others) Charlie Mingus on
Joni Mitchell. Spencer (1981a) describes successful work of this
type with average pupils.

Such ideas as the above may well be stimulating, but they leave
the teacher with the perennial problem of how to develop exciting
individual work, whilst being responsible for a class of twenty and
more pupils. There can be no easy answer to this difficulty, but
one possibility is to remember the importance in pop of the backing
group. Not only does this involve more pupils, but it teaches the
disciplines of pitch, control of tone, timing and phrasing. Since
the importance of pop groups is at least as great as that of individual singers, details are given in all books. Pupils should listen

to such work and so come to understand the role played by backing groups. They should then attempt to learn by imitation
(notation should come later, when the function of backing lines
and their inner logic are understood) and also to find harmonies
or call-and-response phrases of their own as a backing for tunes
that they like. Some description of this approach is to be found
in Lee (1981b).

A further extension of the small-group principle is the approach
suggested by Simon Frith. This is to create 'doo-wop' arrangements
(see SF, DR1), in which the voices take on all the important
functions (tune, bass, etc.), often imitating instruments. This
dispenses with the need for instrumental support.

Finally, we should mention two ways in which large groups of
pupils can be involved, thus solving some of the problems of
classroom management. One is to create several 'sections' working
antiphonally (cf. the practice of big bands). A singer, three
five-voice sections (taking the place of trumpets, trombones and
saxes), a largish rhythm section (five or six pupils), a solo
guitarist and a handful of instrumentalists will account for all but
the largest classes. A second possibility is full-scale choral work,
which also has its place, though it is less of a feature of the
popular tradition outside of the musical theatre. Robins (1976)
gives a stimulating and very practical account of such work.

CRITERIA OF VOICE TONE

One reason for the rejection of popular singing by many classical
musicians is that pop styles differ so markedly in sound from what
is taken to be good tone in conservatories. The classically trained
singer will, of course, often concede that pop singing can be a
pleasant use of the 'natural' voice by talented but untrained performers. Such a view is understandable, but it does not exhaust
possible legitimate ways of looking at vocal music.

In the first place, ethnomusicology has shown that the use of
a term such as 'natural' has to be approached with great care.
Classical vocal style is not the only one in which there is an
insistence upon training, skill in using vocal techniques and the
elimination of elements which are considered unaesthetic. The
difference between styles is hence not one between 'naturalness'
and 'artificiality' but one of emphasis on different potentialities of
the voice. A concrete and highly relevant example from our field
is that of Elvis Presley. Clearly, his sound is not 'good' in a
classical sense; equally clearly his sound is valued highly by
millions. Most important, it is clear from documentary evidence
that, at least at the start of his career, he approached recording
with great singlemindedness, working for many hours on every
detail of his performance. Indeed, despite the myths of spontaneity
created by the popular press, some form of intense self-criticism
seems to be characteristic of many of the most famous popular
singers.

The problem nevertheless remains for the music teacher of how
to incorporate popular singing into his curriculum and how to find
an acceptable role for himself. In part, the latter question is
answered, we believe, in something like the way described by
Spencer (1976b; 1981a; 1981b). What the teacher also needs is
some sort of technical 'checklist' against which he can make comments at appropriate points. Since at the moment such a list does
not exist, the teacher is obliged to invent his own. A valuable
preliminary move in this respect might be to look at Lomax (1968).
This is probably the most noteworthy and comprehensive attempt
by an ethnomusicologist to classify vocal styles. It is not possible
to describe his work in detail here, if only because he lists some
thirty-seven criteria out of which the 'profile' of a song may be
constructed. Some might argue that Lomax is not as useful to
musicians as he might be, because he is primarily concerned with
an examination of the relationship between the song and the culture which created it. Nevertheless, his emphasis on those aspects
of performance which do not emerge from conventional notation
makes his work extremely useful.

POSSIBLE CRITERIA OF ANALYSIS: SOME STARTING-POINTS

1	'Family'	Afro-American or European? North America - Latin America - Caribbean? If North America - black or white tradition?
2	Style	What styles seem to be the basic ones in the opinion of the pop audience? Who are the major artists in a given style (since their work defines the criteria of excellence in that style)?

3	Musical description	As a musician, what seem to you to
		be the basic characteristics of the
		style in terms of:
		(a) pitch: note especially recurrent
		    intervals, note patterns, alter-
		    ations of pitch. What forms of
		    'ornamentation' are typical?
		(b) rhythm: in particular in what
		    ways is the rhythm varied?
		(c) 'expressive techniques': are the
		    notes approached in character-
		    istic ways, e.g. slurs?
		(d) timbre/tone: what is the typical
		    sound, e.g. the country and
		    western 'twang'? In what way
		    is the sound created e.g.
		    falsetto, use of diaphragm?

4 Non-technical factors   Are there crucial non-technical
                           elements in a good performance
                           (see also Lyrics, pp. 63-71).

It is emphasised that the above is in no way exhaustive; it is
meant to act as the starting-point for teachers with no experience
of pop and possibly a limited experience of singing. But we
believe that it at least indicates what might be sensible questions
and comments. (We should perhaps also stress that the above is
an aid to the teacher, who may set about the presentation of his
insights from a totally different angle.)

5 MELODY, HARMONY, COUNTERPOINT AND FORM

These terms, which are so important in the discussion of classical
music that they form whole sections of the syllabus, can be
grouped together in the consideration of Afro-American music,
because the latter tends to focus its attention on the exploitation
of rhythm and timbre. It is thus possible to find pieces of Afro-
American music which, though deemed excellent by most informed
observers, are nevertheless 'weak' if described in the traditional
terms of form, harmony, counterpoint and even melody. (This
point is discussed in Vulliamy, 1976a.)

The terms under discussion have such apparently clear meanings in the conservatory that it is easy to assume that they are
capable of universal application. This is not so, and to act as if
it were is, at the least, likely to render accurate insights into
other musics more difficult to obtain.

It is worth listing just a few of the assumptions which one can
carry over to other musical cultures in which they are unwarranted
or inappropriate.

(1) Harmony: in classical music of the period 1600-1900 approx-
imately, this is concerned with a sense of motion and development.
In other cultures either (a) harmony does not exist, or (b) it is
used for very different purposes. In rock, for example, it is
often conceived as a 'static' repeated element, which is monotonous
to the classical ear but which, like other forms of repetition, is
exciting to the rock listener.

(2) Counterpoint: this is a label which is convenient but which
can be used loosely by classical musicians. For example, there
are obviously important differences between the strict 'note against
note' concept, the music of the polyphonic age, and, say, contrapuntal works in imitation of Bach by nineteenth-century composers.
In Afro-American music 'counterpoint' in its strict sense does
not exist except in pastiche. The music nevertheless has inter-
twining and contrasting strands. But these are conceived of as
manifestations of a total rhythmic structure (see pp. 30-2). There
is at present no satisfactory account of the phenomenon. A basic
perspective might be obtained from works on Latin-American percussion playing (see Latin Percussion Ltd, 1974; Morales, 1949).

(3) Melody: this is a term which is regularly applied to certain
areas of the classical repertoire. But one is unlikely to talk of a
'Palestrina melody' or even of the 'opening melody' of a Beethoven
movement in sonata form. Additionally, there is the problem that
the term is associated with the adjective 'melodious', an epithet
which is highly normative, and is concerned with the judgment

of the aesthetic value of a 'tune' rather than with describing its nature.

In Afro-American music the problem is complicated by the exist-ence of a spectrum of approaches to the main single line of a piece. These vary from the neo-Romantic themes of the American musical to the 'bluesy' line of the soul singer and the speech-like creations of many new wave singers. Thus whenever we are prone to label a piece as 'tuneless' or 'lacking in melody' we should always check that we are clear about the intentions of the com-poser. Punk rockers do not, for better or worse, attempt to sound like Doris Day singing 'Secret Love'. It does not therefore seem very helpful to judge them by such standards. In particular, the nearer one gets to the 'African' end of the spectrum, the less likely is the artist to be concerned with 'melody' in the nineteenth-century or everyday sense.

Useful studies of 'melody' have been made, notably Lee (1970) and Wilder (1972) for 'melody', and Titon (1977) for the Afro-American (blues) line.

(4) Form: this is the term which perhaps causes the greatest difficulties of all. An important reason for this is that for many listeners 'form' is equated with the contrapuntal works of Bach, and with the development of sonata form, notably by Beethoven. Starting from the work of these artists, it has often been argued that Western European classical music is the most highly developed and complex music, because of the virtual non-existence in other musical cultures of forms constructed on the basis of the elabor-ation of motifs in interaction with harmonic movement. This is analogous to arguing that cricket is superior to football because footballers do not demonstrate skill in the use of a bat.

Without in any way wishing to diminish or minimise the value of the works of the classical masters, we can only assert here (on the basis of extensive evidence) that musicians in other cultures have indeed interested themselves in form - meaning by that term the creation of sound patterns according to agreed, but not always explicitly stated, principles. Furthermore some form making has reached a very high degree of sophistication. In the case of Afro-American music Chester (1970) has convincingly argued that form making takes place within what he terms the 'intensional' para-meters of alteration of timbre and rhythmic nuance.

For discussions of the problems of evaluating form see Shepherd et al. (1980, general); Titon (1977, blues); Lee (1972, jazz); Schuller (1968, jazz); Daniélou (1968, Indian); Jones (1959, African); Karpeles (1973, English folk); Sharp (1965, English folk); and Collinson (1966, Scottish).

BASES FOR COURSE CONSTRUCTION

Harmony

Illustrate the use by Afro-American musicians of:

(i) *Traditional harmony* (cycle of fifths, etc.)
use by white musicians: Tin Pan Alley, jazz, country and western, rock'n'roll.
use by black musicians: jazz, rock, soul, blues.
(ii) *Folk modes* Folk, rock, contemporary folk.
(iii) *Contemporary (twentieth-century) harmony* Some rock, jazz-rock, free jazz.

Note:
1 Though it is true to say that in some senses the use of traditional harmony in Afro-American music can be reduced to a few basic progressions, it is important to recognise that crucial distinctions of style are made (a) by added notes and (b) by voicing.

2 Afro-American listeners tend to make an immediate stylistic distinction and with it an aesthetic judgment between styles based on the dominant seventh and those based on folk modes. The comparison of examples from Tin Pan Alley and folk-rock will make this strikingly clear. Rock'n'roll provides an excellent example of a music in transition. Interesting comparisons can be drawn between, say, the traditional harmonies of the ballad singers, Cliff Richard and others, the blues influences found in the work of Haley and Presley, and the use of folk modes, at least occasionally, by artists such as the Everly Brothers.

Substantial progress in developing musicianship can be achieved by:

(a) involvement of pupils on instruments (see Spencer, 1976a; 1976b; 1981a; 1981b);
(b) encouraging pupils to look out for basic changes (denoted by chord symbols) rather than details of part movement (see Comer, 1981a; Burnett, 1981).

Counterpoint

In Afro-American music pupils can come to perceive two layers of motion in the following:

(a) Third Stream experiments of the 1950s, notably the Modern Jazz Quartet and Gerry Mulligan (e.g. 'Gone

Fishin' '). These works follow techniques very close at times to those of the eighteenth century.

(b) Two melodies set against each other. There have been many examples of this technique, especially in Tin Pan Alley music (e.g. Irving Berlin's 'You're Just in Love' from 'Call Me Madam', and the occasional use of Dvorak's 'Humoresque' against 'Swanee River').

(c) Simultaneous improvised soloing in jazz (e.g. Tubby Hayes and the Jazz Couriers) and in rock (Wishbone Ash's earlier numbers).

(d) Use of repeated riff patterns over which another line is played (e.g boogie woogie, big bands, soul, reggae).

(e) Extension of the call-and-response pattern to the point at which there is substantial overlap, giving two virtually continuous though contrasting lines (gospel, blues).

Pupils can easily be brought to exploit their own capacity for working in at least some of these areas, without the need which they have in traditional studies for very technical, paper-based preparation (for examples see Spencer, 1976b; 1981b).

Melody

Pupils will easily recognise the 'spectrum' in this field.
  Possible dimensions of a course are:

'European' melody: (Tin Pan Alley, Duke Ellington)
    (n.b. possible distinctions between European and American, for example operetta writers (Lehar) and American songwriters (Kern, Berlin). Also the differences between 'nineteenth-century' and 'twentieth-century' styles - see Lee, 1970).
Folk' tune': (see EL, BC, black spirituals)
Folk and rock themes: ('melodies' less square cut, more folklike then folk tunes, but more complex in some respects)
Ornamented 'European' and 'folk' lines (jazz, gospel)
Other distinctive types of 'melody' (American teenage-DR1; reggae)
Blues/pentatonic (GV, DR1, DR2, SF)
Jazz themes (bebop) (often motifs are developed in ways reminiscent in technique, but not effect, of European composition - see Lee, 1972)

Outline of possible course linking 'melody' and 'counterpoint'

Term	Week	Topic	Comments
One	1	'European' lines	Get pupils' responses, examine characteristics
	2	Tin Pan Alley	Any differences from 1?

Term	Week	Topic	Comments
	3	Further distinctions	Are there personal styles (Kern, Berlin)?
	4		
	5	Combination of themes	
	6	Folk tunes	take examples from different parts of the world to show versatility of pentatonic scale
	7	Folk and rock tunes	can we classify them, do these classifications go with different styles?
	8		
	9	Distinctive types of tune	American
	10		reggae
	11	Tune making	first steps
	12		

Two   (two weeks each topic)
1   Blues and pentatonic music
2   Call and response
3   Overlap in call and response
4   Riff patterns set against each other
5   Ornamentation (see especially experience of Dene, described in Spencer, 1976b)

The above topics can lead to excellent creative work (see Spencer, 1976a).

Three   (two weeks each topic)
1   Line in Bach
2   Jazz imitations
3   Bop themes
4   Simultaneous soloing

These topics are obviously difficult but are included here for two reasons. First, they can be pursued profitably, when it is possible to work individually with cassettes (see Farmer, 1981). A theme can be broken down rather on the lines used in language laboratory teaching. Second, though much of the teacher's work must be concerned with the needs of the average pupil, there are always those pupils who are capable of much more advanced work. Examples such as the above indicate that study in the Afro-American field is more than capable of standing up to this kind of intellectual and musical challenge. We realise that the topics could well be topics for an undergraduate course; but we are convinced that school pupils should not be under-estimated, and that when guided by a skilful and imaginative teacher, they are capable of *beginning* the process of forming such concepts, and of discussing both these musical topics and the social themes fruitfully, if the ideas are presented in suitable language illustrated by plentiful concrete exemplification.

Form

Two main lines of approach are advocated. First, the tracing of form in traditional European terms:

recognise	themes
	main sections (usually 8 bars), introductions, coda
	phrases (usually two bars)
recognise	cadences
	basic chord sequences
	types of harmony
	use of underlying sequence as basis for improvisation (especially jazz, dub)
identify	call-and-response patterns
	development of large-scale rock works after 1967 (Yes, Genesis, ELP)

Second, we would recommend an approach to description of the music in alternative terms:

rhythm (see above).
timbre (see pp. 56-62).
contrast and tension

Exercises in this type of work - note especially links with singers (Spencer, 1981a) and guitarists (Lee, 1981a)
    Teachers should consider for themselves the value of the ideas of Chester (1970 - discussed in Vulliamy, 1976a) and Keil (1966a).

John Shepherd draws attention to the fact that the above frameworks proceed from the 'European' concept. This is done for the convenience of teachers, who are likely to have to work outwards from their familiarity with such ideas. No superiority is implied, nor is a classroom programme being advocated. There would be much to be said, for example, for beginning right in the heart of the Afro-American tradition, with the work of artists such as James Brown, or the early Rolling Stones.

6 ORCHESTRATION, TONE AND TIMBRE

The above topics have been combined because they all relate to the quality of sound made by musical instruments, as distinct from a concern with pitch or rhythm. Sound colour is possibly the aspect of attentive listening which is most easily perceived and developed. Most people seem to like new and unusual sounds. They can both perceive sounds as sensory experiences and respond to them emotionally. Moreover, sound colour is a dimension of Afro-American music through which styles can immediately be distinguished.

The topic can be approached in various ways. The teacher could for instance lead a project in which pupils 'collect' unusual sound effects. Alternatively, new and traditional uses of the same instrument can be compared. The topic can be approached by the usual 'instrumental family' method (strings, woodwind, percussion etc.) or according to popular groupings (rhythm section, backing group etc.). Again, different styles can be defined by their use of instruments (e.g country and western - steel guitar).

The following system of classification is not prescriptive, but is the one used as the basis of this article:

(a)   the use of instruments in ensemble;
(b)   the basic sound of individual instruments;
(c)   alterations of sound at the level of the individual note.

INSTRUMENTS IN ENSEMBLE

Since its earliest days Afro-American music has differentiated itself from the typical 'classical' sound. This has been inevitable because of the differing emphasis on rhythm, resulting in the creation of the rhythm section. In this respect the effect of the continuous presence of drums cannot be over-stressed. A difference of sound from classical practice also came about because the music has had to fulfil different functions, and notably that of public performance in large halls and noisy circumstances, often as an accompaniment to dancing. It was thus necessary to use instruments to produce volume, and it became possible to exploit volume as a structural function of the music. JS describes the process in its earlier stages, and GV shows how early jazz bands still used some of the traditional classical instruments, because at first they had also to perform typical nineteenth-century dance music (see EL).

Of great importance before rock'n'roll was the use of brass instruments and the saxophone. The process of the combination of these instruments into sections is described by JS and GV.

In parallel with these developments was a stress on new sounds - in the first instance to produce novelty products offered on a highly competitive market. This is directly related to the emergence of a capitalist mode of musical production, and the creation and exploitation of new media described by JS. But we would argue that the search for novelty did not only produce moments of profound banality, such as the use of the Swanee Whistle by Louis Armstrong's Hot Five, and the tubular bells by Paul Whiteman. Arrangers also produced a steady succession of minor insights into orchestration which can make pop music a joy to listen to. Many a record has been sold by an imaginative sound effect of this sort (we take it that saleability does not automatically entail lack of quality). This type of musical product helped to create a system of values in the audience which attached high value to the sensory experience of sound colours.

We advocate that the teacher should keep a lookout for effects which will enhance his lessons and tape them. As a starting-point we suggest:

development of sections	King Oliver, Fletcher Henderson, Count Basie;
novelty in dance bands of the 1920s, and 1930s	Paul Whiteman, Ambrose, Savoy Orpheans;
individual sound of band	Duke Ellington, Glenn Miller, Stan Kenton;
emergence of the electric guitar	Charlie Christian, Django Reinhardt, rock'n'roll.

In the 1960s the question of tone colour became a major pre-occupation with rock musicians (DR2). Of particular importance were the use of the electric organ, of guitar effects (e.g. fuzz) and of the synthesiser. Wherever possible the teacher should look for two versions of the same song and so illustrate the degree to which the original conception was not only in terms of line, but of particular instrumental combinations and keys. It is not a generally held view, but we feel that few reworkings of the rock songs of the Beatles and Bob Dylan are anywhere near as success-ful as the originals, because these were so much conceived in terms of specific sound colours.

Another major development of the 1960s was the emergence of recording as a form of musical creation which differed in important respects from all other musical phenomena. Before recording, popular music could only be a live experience. Even after the invention of recording, the quality of reproduction was poor for many years. Additionally, recording had a complex relationship to live music (described in JS) in which it acted by proxy for live performances, and as a form of publicity for them. Recording also created new physical media (radio and gramophone records) which in turn led to new mental attitudes (e.g. the star system). During the period before about 1960, recording tended to bear the same relationship to live music as a snapshot does to reality. However, the development of electronic technology made it possible for rock artists to control their recordings, just as they sought to control the commercial process (see DR2). By means of over-dubbing it became possible to take responsibility for the greater part and even the whole of the product. It then became possible to compose at the tape recorder. A few outstanding examples of music of this type are the Beatles' 'Sergeant Pepper's Lonely Hearts Club Band', Pink Floyd's 'The Piper at the Gates of Dawn', and Mike Oldfield's 'Tubular Bells'.

A concern with colour is not only to be found in such examples of 'total composition'. Even at a semi-professional level any record-ing engineer will work with the group to 'get a sound' - that is, to find a balance of volume and timbre which is the basic 'canvas' upon which the group will work. In such situations the participants have in no way been 'dehumanised' by the machines. Though it may not always be taken, the option is very much open for men not only to be the masters of the machines, but to use them in a very creative fashion. Indeed, electronic devices increase the number of variables in composition, and hence the number of creative possibilities; the machine renders more complex the choices which have to be made. Furthermore the act of 'producing' the record (i.e. of making judgments about the use of devices and about the end result) is also in many cases highly creative. Thus the sound engineer, formerly a 'mere technician' takes on a crucial creative function. Since electronic devices permit one to control very exactly the relative volume and tone of subsidiary instruments as well as such factors as echo, bass weighting and so on, there are a large number of decisions which the participants must make. It is on the strength of such decisions that this type of work can and must be judged. A comprehensive evaluation could not omit consideration of such factors.

The work of Malcolm Nicholls (1976) shows just how far this process can be taken with average pupils. Like him we would recommend that pupils should both listen to and discuss records as a distinct medium of musical expression, and should supple-ment such work by practical explorations of the tape recorder and its possibilities. (For detailed guidance on work with tape recorders see Dwyer, 1975.)

THE SOUND OF INDIVIDUAL INSTRUMENTS

Any popular artist who wishes to make more than a basic living has to look for an individual sound. Though there is undoubtedly a steady stream of work for anonymous but skilled craftsmen, the greatest rewards seem invariably to go to artists who strike the public as being 'original'. This is not the place to discuss in detail what 'originality' may be, but it is certain that many artists (Sinatra, McCartney, Hendrix, Ellington) are instantly recognisable by their individual sound. This search for individualised sound is, as we have seen earlier, a fundamental concern of Afro-American music. The teacher should ask his pupils to bring in examples of what they consider to be distinctive and original sounds, and should do so himself. The books in this series provide an adequate guide. It may be difficult for pupils to describe in words what they hear, and why they feel it is different. This is less vital than that they should demonstrate a capacity for recognising differences, and develop the habit of looking for them.

Time should also be given to practical music making in which the differences between individuals can be noted. This can happen at a very early stage since concepts of the process of music making differ widely between untutored performers. Many teachers may be concerned that such activity might militate against what they deem to be their primary function of fostering a 'correct' tone. This is undoubtedly necessary if the task of the performer is to reproduce faithfully what has been judged to be good in the past. Moreover, one cannot dismiss lightly the concern of teachers about encouraging 'bad habits'. We nevertheless feel that before pupils acquire such skill, 'natural' differences can be noted, and perhaps some insight be given into the different natures and purposes of 'reproductory' and 'personalised' musics. (More detailed discussion of the question of 'good habits' in relation to the teaching of the guitar and singing are given in Vulliamy and Lee, 1981.)

Almost certainly pupils will be aware in some measure of the differences of tone colour between different guitarists. Thus the sound colour of the work of George Benson differs from that of his contemporaries both because of the techniques which he uses, and because of the type of guitar on which he plays.

In view of the generally low esteem in which percussion is held in classical training, the teacher is strongly urged to listen especially attentively to drummers, who habitually spend a great deal of time and effort on selecting the sounds, both of each unit of the kit, and of the kit as a whole. Very clear differences of this type can be distinguished, and when this has been done, the listener's appreciation of the music will undoubtedly have been enhanced.

SOUND COLOUR AND THE INDIVIDUAL NOTE

As Chester (1970) suggests Afro-American musicians express themselves not through a concentration on the variation of motifs and harmonic movement, but on rhythmic nuance, and the subtle variation of the sound of the individual note. One might at first incline to use terms such as 'interpretation', 'expression' or 'ornamentation' to label the latter process, but to do so would be

misleading. Such terms carry an implication that there is an
essential musical work whose meaning is brought out by the addition of such elements. Chester's point is that in Afro-American
music, these elements are not additions, but are at the centre of
the musical system. They are the very materials with which the
performer/composer operates from the start.

Pupils should thus be brought at every point to recognise that
the recurrent interest of popular artists in all styles has been
in the shaping of the notes - in sculpting notes out of the vast
resource of 'pure sound', as it were. This can be heard as clearly
in the playing of Louis Armstrong as in that of Eric Clapton, and
in the singing of Bing Crosby as in that of David Bowie. For us,
possibly the most outstanding exponent of this dimension of music
was Jimi Hendrix. His conception of 'The Star Spangled Banner'
seems to indicate a whole new realm of music in which clear-cut,
grid-like structures are abandoned in favour of a journey through
a sea of sound.

The significance of this dimension of Afro-American music has
not been appreciated fully by critics trained in a concept of music
which has largely been moulded by the Western European tradition.
In the latter, timbre is relatively standardised because it is not
controllable by the composer through notation. Hence there is
virtually nothing written on the topic. The nearest articles we
know of those of Keil (1966a) and Chester (1970). But we would
recommend the guitar tutors of Green Note Music (1973) and
B.B. King (1973) as a useful attempt to classify these phenomena
with relation to the electric guitar. It is noteworthy that in both
cases it has been necessary to issue an accompanying record.

This fact of reliance on records points to a major difficulty in
discussing this topic, which is that we are dealing with essentially
aural phenomena, which are not really susceptible to any useful
form of notation. Wishart (1980a) argues that this innate imperma-
nence (at least in the age before recording) meant that higher
esteem was given to elements in music which can be given a more
permanent and definitive form through written notation.

On the other hand, the educational advantages of studying this
aspect of the music are considerable. First, the listener develops
a high degree of aural sensitivity, and an intense attention to
the morphology of notes. Second, many difficulties of less literate
pupils are obviated. The possibilities which emerge when the con-
straint of notation is abandoned are illustrated by Spencer (1976b).
We feel that Spencer's work, like that of Labov in language (1974),
demonstrates that there is no necessary correlation between
'intelligence' or 'achievement' on the one hand, and literacy
(musical or verbal) on the other. A third advantage is that whereas
the performance of a whole piece, though desirable, takes much
preparation, all pupils can at once approach instruments to play
individual notes, and to explore those notes as sounds. No ability
as a guitar player is needed in order to experiment with 'bending'
a single note. (There are clearly useful links here with certain
types of 'avant garde' approach; we recommend Paynter and Aston

(1970) and Wishart (1974) as excellent starting-points in this respect.)

No detailed syllabus is given here. The phenomenon is universal in popular music, and the teacher is advised to collect his own examples. Since the field is as yet unexplored by scholars, no definitive course structure could be given. We would only recommend listening to the music, discussing very short passages, the illustration of individual techniques by the teacher or by a pupil who plays, and periods of exploration by pupils. Usually more than one of these approaches would be used in a given lesson.

A NOTE ON IMPROVISATION

When an artist alters notes in the ways outlined in the last section he is engaged in a form of improvisation. A few words about this often misunderstood term are therefore appropriate here.

In performance a blues player extemporises variations of stock 'melodic patterns' or themes; such variations are created in the fashion described above, and notably by changes of rhythm and timbre.

At one remove from this type of variation is that described by John Shepherd (JS, ch. 8). In such music the singer does not vary material which is taken from an aurally acquired body of folk themes; instead he varies European-style compositions which have been disseminated through notation. Thus a striking fact about the average pop-song sheet or arrangement is its simplicity relative to a symphonic score. This is because, to the musician who understands the aurally transmitted conventions of popular music, it is unnecessary to restate them in writing. Moreover, it is undesirable to prescribe performance too closely, since it is in an individual performance that value will be found, and in which complexity (of 'interpretation' and rhythm) of reworking of the simple sheet-music skeleton will take place.

The 'interpretation' and 'ornamentation' of a given part is a process which can become increasingly complex (as in New Orleans jazz) until finally (as in 'swing' solos) the original theme disappears entirely in favour of a new improvised line, in a manner in some respects similar to the creation of 'divisions' in the sixteenth and seventeenth centuries. This step having been taken, the jazz concept of a chorus arises. As in a chaconne, the length and harmonic basis of the piece remain essentially unchanged, while the soloist extemporises on top. In the urban blues, such extemporisation is concerned predominantly with rhythm and timbre; in jazz there is also a concern with cross rhythmic patterns and with thematic invention.

With the more sophisticated pupil, teachers could do some very exciting and valuable work by studying the nature of the transition between 'ornamented melody' and 'new variation' (notably in jazz), by studying the extent to which ideas are developed over a longer period (as in the work of Charlie Parker), and the extent to which in rock solos musicians can be divided into those who string together a set of acceptable 'licks', and those who, like Hendrix, create new unified ideas on a much larger scale.

A further extension of the concept of improvisation came in 'free form' jazz, and in the more 'progressive' rock groups such as Henry Cow, Etron Fou and This Heat. At this point the unifying basis of the repeated chord sequence is cast aside, leaving the players the freedom to evolve the form of their music spontaneously. In modern jazz we also find a great interest in extended solos, unrestricted by an underlying form, by such players as Sonny Rollins and the current New York school of saxists.

More detailed discussions of how improvisation works are to be found in Lee (1970; 1972) and Vulliamy and Lee (1976).

7 POPULAR SONG LYRICS

THE MUSICIAN AND WORDS

It has been argued above that popular music is for the most part
popular *song*. It thus follows that the music teacher should
include the study of lyrics as part of his course. Such a sugges-
tion is likely to jar a little at first, since musicians have a tendency to see themselves either as instrumentalists or singers but
not as lyricists, and their training reinforces this. But we draw
attention to the fact that in many other cultures the tasks of
poet and musician are part of the same activity. In Africa, the
praise singer must both play and improvise verses. In earlier
European culture poets such as Homer and Virgil refer, even
though it may well be metaphorically, to their work as 'song'.
Classical musicians were continuously concerned with the setting
of words, sacred and secular - the words of Thomas Morley are
regularly quoted on this matter. We therefore argue that, though
collaboration between music teachers and English teachers can
only be advantageous to both parties, the musician, to be a complete musician has to have a working knowledge of verse making
and setting.
   The above remarks lead us to a more fundamental consideration
regarding the difference between 'poetry' as conceived in Europe
over the past few centuries and the lyrics of popular songs. It
is fair to say that to a great extent the various forms of art in
Europe have become separated: by and large poetry is not linked
with music or with drama. In contrast to this, the popular lyric
is largely meaningless, if it is not considered in conjunction with
music, with performance, and with context. In the next few pages
we shall develop this point. However, before doing so we propose
briefly to digress.

THE THEMATIC APPROACH

Popular lyrics can be seen quite simply as one more, often very
lively, way of drawing the attention of pupils to themes which
may be historical, social, emotional or moral. There is now a
wealth of material containing lyrics of all periods, which can lead
on from the start made by our series. Every writer quotes lyrics,
some (DR1, BC) very extensively. BC is an excellent lead in to
some of the more 'poetic' areas of popular lyrics; DR1, on the other
hand, relates them very clearly to social forces and to context.

A range of approaches suggest themselves. The teacher can get
the class to compare the main stages of lyric development: folk
music (EL); Victorian (EL); Tin Pan Alley (JS); rock'n'roll (DR1);
1960s' rock (DR2); 1970s' new wave (DR2). Very quickly, important differences of tone and subject-matter will be noted. The
omission of explicitly sexual references in Tin Pan Alley music,
and the heavy sentimentality of the Victorians are perhaps
especially striking (see Lee, 1970). Such characteristics should
be related to historical factors, for example the self-imposed
system of censorship used by commercial interests after about
1930. This suggests another use for popular lyrics, which is as
data and support material for historical projects. A term of
historical study can often be brought to life by a short concert
of appropriate music, especially if it can be put on in period
dress.

Lyrics can also give rise to the consideration of a range of social
topics. To ask what attitudes a given song reflects inevitably
leads to a comparison between those attitudes and our own views.
The use of innuendo by Marie Lloyd (EL) is a far cry from the
sexual directness of some recent songs. The celebration of alcohol
in drinking songs contrasts greatly with the self-absorbed imagery
of psychedelia.

Young people should also be led towards a recognition of the
contrasts between a popular culture which appealed to all, and
the youth cultures of the second half of the twentieth century.
It is useful also to consider whether earlier manifestations of
youth culture have any meaning to today's young people, and
what they consider to be the gains and losses of modern industrial
societies in contrast to the much more homogeneous cultures of
which folk music was a product.

POP LYRICS AND POETRY

It was stated in the first paragraph that poetry has tended to
become separated from the other arts, and certainly from music.
Similarly, despite the work of Eliot and Fry, poets in recent times
have been little involved with drama.

Poetry, in the sense that we use it to refer to the work of
Donne, Pope or Keats, was a sophisticated product provided by
and for the educated upper classes. Increasingly it became transmitted through print. Following the arguments of Shepherd (1980),
it would seem that almost inevitably poetry became more and more
a matter for detached reflection on the part of both writer and
audience, which came to accept and value increasingly oblique
ways of writing, subtle metaphors, and deeply embedded meanings
in complex conceptual networks. With the increasing popularity
of the ideals of Romanticism, it also became increasingly important
for the poet to establish his 'originality' and beyond that his
'genius'. By such criteria, no popular lyricist has any hope of
being seen as an artist. When pop lyrics are read in silence they

are usually apparently simple, direct, and lacking in subtlety of
technique or vocabulary. Such differences are due to historical
developments which have led both to a separation of poetry and
song, and to a tendency to evaluate the lyrics of the latter in
terms of the former.

THE IMPORTANCE OF CONTEXT

As we have seen, poetry became an independent form of art which
could, by means of print, maintain an existence independent of
its creator. We can possess books of poetry and read them alone,
in silence. This has never happened to popular song, in which
sheet music bears little resemblance to the actuality of living pop
music. Pop singing is a series of performances, and performances
can only take place in a context. We thus return to a pervasive
theme of this book: the importance of context.
   The notion of context can help us to see the error in comparing
poetry and pop lyrics. Popular and folk lyrics are designed for
all - not just for the educated or those brought up to recognise
the conventions of a culture which is not universal. Popular lyrics
are made for people with limited leisure, and no formal introduction
to the conventions of the 'high' arts. Such lyrics need first and
foremost to be immediately understood; information must be conveyed instantly and without the need for reflection on the part
of the audience. This is further made necessary by the fact that
folk and popular lyrics are sung, not read - they are a branch
of oral literature, which has its own strengths and limitations.

THE LANGUAGE OF POPULAR LYRICS

A first criterion of popular lyrics is thus that the diction (choice
of vocabulary) needs to be suited to the audience. It needs to
reflect that language used by the audience. It is not a criticism
of popular songs to say that their lyrics are 'colloquial', 'Ameri-
canised' or 'ungrammatical' since such epithets (which in fact
are often linguistically extremely imprecise) reflect in part the
language habits of the audience. In the classroom such lyrics
can be a useful starting-point for the consideration of the nature
and use of language (the works of Eric Partridge could be very
useful here). In the case of reggae one would also have to look
at the whole question of West Indian forms of English, dialects
and creoles.
   However, all art, including the lyrics of popular songs, is to
some degree conventionalised. Thus pupils should be asked to
consider whether the language of popular songs really is 'the
language of ordinary men', even in contemporary lyrics, in relation
to which their language sensitivities are most highly developed.
Among the topics which might be looked at are:

To what extent is a lyric 'universal'? Is it likely to appeal to a
large number of people all over the world (JS suggests that
this was a strength of Tin Pan Alley)? Have older lyrics a last-
ing appeal?

Is the use of language witty or ironic? (Pupils are quick to
detect misreadings of lyrics by critics of the Holbrook type,
who see only the literal meaning of the printed text, and are
unaware of contextual indicators of irony. EL notes this type
of factor in the work of Marie Lloyd. Irony is also an important
feature of the songs of the 1960s and 1970s. Dave Rogers points
out this type of misinterpretation in Vulliamy and Lee (1976)).

Is the language used an example of 'in talk' (e.g. about drugs
in 1960s' rock, or about 'Babylon' in reggae)?

What is our attitude to 'corny' Tin Pan Alley lyrics? Did people
really believe them (pupils could ask grandparents)? For
example, it could be argued that in escapist films, both actors
and audiences are very aware that what they are involved in is
a fiction.

In a highly conventionalised form, what constitutes value? For
example, with a little humour, both teacher and pupils can discover what you can't say in a rock'n'roll lyric (e.g. 'My year's
accounts show a negative balance'). And some of the games
suggested by Wishart (1974) show how difficult it is to innovate
within very strict limits (e.g. to find new ways to articulate
one note).

SURFACE AND HIDDEN MEANING

The language of poetry and of pop song lyrics has a 'surface'
meaning which can be deduced directly from the text. However,
we need to recognise that language can and does operate on
several levels simultaneously, and can thus carry other meanings
which are not obvious. The case of irony cited above is a case in
point. Anyone who recognises the irony realises that there is a
conflict between what is actually said, and what is meant. More
generally, any group of people uses language specific to that
group, in which important aspects of what is being communicated
are unstated, or implicit. Such language contains referents which
are obvious to those who share the same linguistic environment
(but not to outsiders), or which are supplied by non-verbal means,
notably by such factors as gesture, tone of voice, or assumed
common knowledge.
   As a specific example of this process, we quote the fact that in
Edward Lee's first book (1970, pp. 242-3) he argued that the
following lines of the Beatles were banal:

Well she was just seventeen,
You know what I mean. . . .

He was glad to receive a comment from Alan Byrne, who pointed
out that in view of the nature of the song, and the history of the
Beatles' career, he felt that the song was cross-referring to Chuck
Berry. Such a reference was rich in unstated associations to the
audience. It evoked memories of Berry, his music, and the good
times associated with it. It did so at a time when rock'n'roll
seemed destroyed by commercialism, and when the Beatles saw
themselves as rebelling against the constraints of the adult world
(see DR2). The reference also established a link between singers
and audience. Those who got the reference were clearly of the
same social group, a recognition which was in itself gratifying.
In this light the apparently banal second line becomes very
logical; it could be pointed up by appropriate non-verbal means
(a wink or something of the sort).
    Various objections might be raised to the above interpretation.
It may be argued, for example, that this is a very slight foun-
dation on which to build a very big edifice. We would reply that
such examples could be multiplied many times. Or one might argue
that no handful of words bears such extensive and cumbersome
interpretation. This is to fail to understand the nature of language,
and particularly that words are in many ways a form of shorthand;
they are summaries of our experience, and like any summary are
capable of re-expansion. Additionally, though live events strike
us instanteously, their impact may be very complex. We can only
analyse such impact over a period of time, explicitly, and in
many more words.
    The reader might also argue that if he needs this degree of
knowledge of the popular world, the use of such lyrics in the
classroom is not for him, a teacher with neither the time nor the
interest to acquire such a depth of understanding. We return to
a theme we have stated often before, that the teacher needs underlying concepts, attitudes and teaching skills so as to provide a
structure for worthwhile communication. Pupils bring their knowledge, which is considerable, and which they do not necessarily
realise they have. The teacher helps them to articulate and reflect
upon it, to see what they know from new perspectives. But because
the pupil is interested, and is genuinely being consulted, he tends
to become motivated and to grow in self-esteem.

THE RELATION BETWEEN WORDS AND MUSIC

It is easy to forget that a popular lyric (or indeed any other
lyric) is not merely a postcard verse, but is one element in a song.
The relationship between the words and the music is thus crucial.
On the one hand, there is the 'contrapuntal' movement of the
phrasing of the verbal line, which can unite with, or be set
against, the movement of the melodic line. Additionally, there are

factors such as the suitability of the words to the rhythm, and vice versa. For example, a very quick moving line tends to be a feature of comic songs (e.g. in the music hall) and to sound ludicrous in a serious love ballad. Again, there is the mellifluous nature (or otherwise) of the sound of the words. For example, it might be difficult to set 'The asthmatic toad denounced the gnu.'

We must also ask whether rhyme has any function. Songs of the Tin Pan Alley type tend to exhibit very sophisticated uses of pun, internal rhyme and other traditional poetic effects, which give the music a very urbane, mocking tone. Again, as in a good eighteenth-century couplet, rhyme often strengthens the sense of expectation and completion of meaning. Finally, we have the questions of the type of melody and harmony chosen, and whether the accompaniment is appropriate. Film makers such as Claude Chabrol are very aware of the way in which a carefully chosen accompaniment can foreshadow a coming event, or underline elements which are not in the area of primary focus (i.e. what is happening on the screen or in the lyric).

The above may seem to be an overstatement for mere popular lyrics. We reply that such a criticism reveals prejudiced opinions not based on close listening or reflection. There is no doubt that the best popular artists have been aware of such factors and have exploited them. We can too easily forget that, however lacking in artifice a popular performance may seem, professional artists are people who use a medium to create audience responses; in this they differ from the adolescent who writes 'therapeutic' poetry to express and relieve personal feelings.

We should perhaps say that we take it for granted that the teacher is not being urged to walk into a class of unmotivated adolescents and give a lecture on Internal Rhyme and the Cult of Sophistication in the Music of Cole Porter. We do not confuse activities appropriate to the teacher during the preparation of classes with the act of teaching. Teaching bears the same relation to what has been said above as does performance to rehearsal for an actor. What we have been indicating are criteria by which a teacher can decide what work to do and how to evaluate it. That very good work of this type is feasible is shown very clearly by the accounts of Spencer (1976b) and Nicholls (1976).

PERFORMANCE

The above remarks do not exhaust the possible areas in which we should look for the 'meaning' of pop lyrics. As was mentioned earlier, meaning can be conveyed by non-verbal means.

Popular songs are designed for performance. As a consequence they can be seen as a species of drama. We must thus take account of the appearance of the artist, in order to know what is being projected by codes of dress (for comment on this matter Jefferson (1976) is worth reading). It is important to know what Marie

Lloyd looked like (see EL); the same is true of Elvis Presley, and especially Gene Vincent (DR1). Singers also use non-verbal means such as gesture and facial expression. Young people are very aware of these factors and are capable of very perceptive parodies.

There is still a further dimension of interpretation in a perform-ance, however, which is that the artist creates an artificial per-sonality for a transient event. Dave Rogers draws attention to the importance of this in the work of David Bowie (DR2). It might be argued that these are complex points, which is in some sense true. But the audience know full well that it is seeing an 'act' - possibly not to recognise this would be a sign of incipient insanity. And pupils will be familiar enough with accounts of the lives of artists which conflict with their stage personality (the rebel Mick Jagger spends his time with the rich he once condemned). Possibly a reason for the continuing popularity of such newspaper articles is not merely scandal, but the puzzlement many of us experience in relating the world as it is presented in the media (whether art or adverts) and as it is in our everyday life.

CONCLUSIONS

The above remarks have attempted to indicate the dangers in applying the traditional criteria of literary criticism to popular lyrics. Poetry is a form which can exist independently of the act of creation, and which enjoys the advantages and constraints of being presented through print. Pop lyrics, on the other hand, are largely inseparable from a total live experience. Our approach must thus be different. In particular, we must expect directness, and simplicity of language, but a great complexity of 'hidden' meaning. This meaning can only be perceived by examining the context and the mode of presentation. There will be a dramatic element in the performance of pop songs; and of course, as in other forms of music, there will be various forms of interplay between words and music.

A POSSIBLE COURSE

It is not possible or desirable to prescribe a course for work of this kind, but we would suggest that a block of ten or twelve lessons is needed to make progress. Elements which should go into such a course are:

Obtain sheet music and see an original performance (a film is possible). Compare ways in which the two media differ in what they present to us.

Historical study - songs from a given period. Background data (as project). Attempt to build up an idea of the preoccupations of the time (e.g. in the nineteenth century, the emphasis on drunkenness, temperance movements, licensing of music halls, gin palaces etc.).

Thematic study (e.g. the treatment of love in different periods).

Collection of songs from one period (e.g. rock'n'roll). What characteristics emerge? Themes, conventions, clichés.

Youth music now and then. What themes are omitted/included? What other factors besides musical style identified the youth movement?

The language of the songs: slang/dialect/creole; cliché/irony/ wit; rhyme/metre.

Link of words with music - problems, failures, successes.

Performance - importance of facial expression, gesture, dress, presentation of 'image'. What is the real person like?

The latter three subjects are better studied in passing during a project or creative work.
  A one-term project might be 'The 1930s' (follow up reading, JS, GV):

Week 1 See musical film.
     2 Discuss effect of film; look at words in sheet music, discuss differences of medium.
     3 Historical background sketched by teacher - pictures, slides, events.
     4 Albums of songs distributed to small groups - look for themes, recurrent vocabulary, images.
     5 Young people of the time. Slides, accounts. Differences from today.
     6 Records and performance by teacher. Attempt to arouse the enthusiasm of the class and get the spirit of the time, if only in parody. Possibly an older visitor talks about how it felt to be alive at the time.
     7 First steps towards performance. 'Inspirational' class leading to allotment of tasks, responsibility for costumes, possible exhibition of pictures and objects. Role play into situations. Dance brought in if possible.
     8 Songs selected, begin rehearsal.
     9 Attempt to write songs in the style. Comments on the musical characteristics, language (see Spencer, 1976b, and especially the accompanying tape to the book 'Pop Music in School' for approaches to such comment).
    10 If needed, detailed technical guidance, more ideas.
    11 Rehearsal, comment on gesture etc.
    12 Final preparations.
    13 Performance.

It should, however, be borne in mind that unless the pupils have done a fair amount of work outside the class, the 'concert' would of course be very informal and unpolished. Also, the above scheme is not to be taken too literally; it would, for example, be easily capable of expansion to double the length of time. Moreover, such work needs to be flexibly handled, even though it should generate a very definite internal discipline of its own. But two points are being made through the scheme. First, it is felt best to offer teachers a range of ideas, from which they can select. Second, to show that if we do not allow ourselves to be too concerned with the standards of public performance, a great deal of ground can be covered, and much insight into music may be given in a short time. For a demonstration of this with regard to the creation of pop arrangements see Comer, 1981a.

8 YOUTH CULTURE

The phenomenal growth in the consumption of pop music in the last few decades has drawn the attention of sociologists to the importance of youth as a separate social category. The origins of the post-war youth culture are often traced to the mid-1950s' explosion of rock'n'roll and the emergence of the 'teenager' (as 1950s' parlance had it). Dave Rogers's 'Rock'n'roll' captures the mood of that time well. Teenagers came to be viewed as a distinct group with their own tastes in music and fashion and their own very distinctive spending habits. They also came increasingly to be viewed as a 'problem' by the mass media, particularly when they formed themselves into distinctive subcultural groups like the teddy boys. An excellent example of a study documenting the rise of such subcultural groups and the reaction of the media to them is Cohen (1973).

A number of explanations were given for the rise of the teenager in the 1950s. One was the argument that the greater affluence of post-war Britain had been shared by young people, especially as a result of the increasing demand for teenage labour. The money gained from teenage employment was spent not on normal 'adult' goods, like furniture or consumer durables or houses, but on a narrow range of teenage interests like records, clothes and means of transport. This view is crystallised in Abrams's (1959) comment 'one gets distinctive teenage spending for distinctive teenage ends in a distinctive teenage world.'

Another common explanation for the rise of a post-war teenage culture was the dramatic growth of education, both at secondary and university level, in the 1950s and 1960s. A larger number of young people were spending an increasing proportion of their time in institutions designed specifically for young people. This was a frequent theme in American sociologists' accounts, like that of Coleman (1961):

> The American high school pupil is cut off from the rest of society, forced inwards towards his own age group. With his fellows he comes to constitute a small society, one that has its most important interactions within itself, and maintains only a few threads of connections with the outside adult society.

If the 1950s saw the decade of the teenager, the 1960s became the era of youth culture. Dave Rogers in his book 'Rock Music' traces the way in which the Beatles' music of the early 1960s came to epitomise an age of supposedly classless (and affluent) youth.

Pop musicians themselves saw their role as a spokesman for youth, as with the Who's famous single, 'My Generation':

> People try to put us down
> Just because we get around
> Things they do look awful cold
> Hope I die before I get old.
> This is my generation, baby. . . .
> (Fabulous Music, 1965).

The late 1960s saw a big boost in the focus on youth via the growth of a youth counterculture, together with student protests, both of which were seen at the time as the logical extension of the earlier moulding of new attitudes in the younger generation. Brian Càrroll's 'Contemporary Folk Song' illustrates the important connections between contemporary folk music on the one hand, and student protest movements against the Vietnam war and the campaign for civil rights, on the other. Dave Rogers's discussion of rock music in the 1960s also demonstrates the close connection between the more progressive styles of rock music and hippies, flower power and the underground. This was the era of large open-air rock festivals, like that of Woodstock, and the talk was of a new youth culture (described by Neville (1971) as 'classless, international and alive') which would change society. Sometimes this was seen in overtly radical terms, as in the influential book by Reich (1972):

> Always before, young people felt themselves tied more to their immediate situations than to a generation. But now an entire culture, including music, clothes and drugs, began to distinguish youth. As it did, the message of consciousness went with it. Consciousness is capable of changing and of destroying the Corporate State, without violence, without seizure of political power, without overthrow of any existing group of people.

The naivety of such a view became increasingly apparent in the 1970s and again Dave Rogers's 'Rock Music' shows the ways in which any radicalism inherent in the late 1960s' youth movement became defused, partly through over-commercialisation and partly through a lack of identification with the interests of ordinary working-class youth. It became evident that an emphasis on the teenager, and later on youth culture, had been misleading in that it obscured the fact that an equally important shaper of adolescents' values and attitudes was the social class background of those involved. Young people are sharply differentiated into different subcultural groups and their distinctiveness is largely shaped by the social class background of the participants. This is one of the themes of the sociological survey reported in Murdock and Phelps (1973). They were interested in the ways in which the mass media influence the experience of schooling and the relationships between teachers' and pupils' attitudes to, and use of, the media. The study was based on a 1970 questionnaire survey of teachers and pupils in ninety English secondary schools of various types, together with more intensive case studies based on participant observation in ten of the schools, where both teachers and pupils could be interviewed in depth.

One of the main conclusions arising from the survey is that pupils from different social class and neighbourhood backgrounds and with different attitudes to school approach the mass media in different ways, and in particular have very different tastes in pop music. More specifically, it was found that for working-class pupils and particularly the early leavers in the lowest streams of secondary schools, the main preferences were for reggae and soul records, together with motown performers and 'hard rock' groups. Actual and prospective sixth-formers, on the other hand, preferred progressive rock music (most of which was to be found on LPs rather than singles), having changed their allegiances from the mass pop of the Top Twenty to such progressive rock music some time between the second and fourth years of secondary schooling. Frith's 1972 survey of 14- to 18-year-olds at a comprehensive school in Keighley, Yorkshire, reported in chapter 3 of 'The Sociology of Rock' (1978), comes to a broadly similar conclusion. Such evidence has led some sociologists to question more conventional interpretations of youth cultures and to make a plea that social class should be reinstated as a crucial factor in the sociology of youth. For example, Murdock and McCron argue this strongly in chapters in both Hall et al. (1976) and Mungham and Pearson (1976) - two useful books, which focus upon the question of whether youth culture is primarily a youth or class phenomenon. Murdock and McCron point out how youth culture groups have always been very strong reflections of their adult social class cultures. Thus, at the time, hippies and the counterculture in the late 1960s were interpreted as an extreme form of the generation gap. However, in retrospect we can see how they were partly an elaboration of certain middle-class values - 'doing your own thing' reflecting a middle-class emphasis on individualism and self-expression. What tended to go largely unobserved at the time was the fact that the majority of working-class youth viewed the counterculture with emotions ranging from lack of interest to outright hostility - such hostility being expressed in youth cults totally opposed to the hippies. The skinheads of the early 1970s were the expression of a working-class distaste for the trendy radicalism of much middle-class youth. As such, the skinheads, like other working-class groups before them (the teds, or later the rockers), held deep-seated, traditional working-class values - a stress on masculinity and physical toughness, group solidarity, an us/them philosophy and a total intolerance of anything 'queer' or 'weird'. The punk explosion of the mid-1970s, and the consequent new wave in rock music, is simply the latest in this long line of working-class reactions against more established youth styles. As the 'Sunday Times' put it:

The punk movement is primarily born of the unemployed, bored and frustrated teenager. They are contemptuous of hippies, drugs, long hair, love, successful rock stars, flashy clothes and all the usual trappings of established pop music.

Whatever one's interpretations of the causes of youth culture, sociological research has always shown the vital role that allegiance to particular styles of pop plays in such subcultural styles. The most detailed sociological study of the involvement of youth cultures in music is Willis's 'Profane Culture' (1978). He focuses upon two particular youth subcultures: motor bike boys and hippies. Rock'n'roll is the music of the former and progressive rock that of the latter. Through detailed participant observation of the lifestyles of each group and through an analysis of each musical style, Willis suggests what it is about the particular musical style that has an attraction for each lifestyle respectively. Another book that gives special prominence to the role of music in post-war youth cultures is Hebdige (1979). By exploring the current links between punk and reggae, Hebdige argues that the interrelations between black and white subcultures are far more important than is generally recognised.

One of the limitations of much sociological and journalistic writing in this area is that it only considers specific youth cultures (and often deviant ones) at the expense of the more 'ordinary' teenager. An interesting exception is Mungham's chapter reporting a study of youth in large dance halls of the Mecca ballroom variety. He (Mungham and Pearson, 1976) concludes:

Through a study of episodes in the provision of a mass leisure facility for 'respectable' working-class youth, I have tried to illustrate the sheer ordinariness of this corner of 'youth culture'. They revealed themselves to me as conservative and quiescent; a group who, measured in terms of their work, leisure and minimal aspirations, demonstrated, at every turn a continuity with the world of their parents' generation.

Another limitation has been the almost exclusive concern with males at the expense of females. Here McRobbie and Garber's chapter on Girls and Subcultures (Hall et al., 1976) is a rare exception.

Finally, a very useful summary of the different perspectives on youth and music is given in chapters 2 and 3 of Frith (1978).

SOME TEACHING SUGGESTIONS

One of the most successful classroom projects on this theme is an attempt to replicate the kind of survey carried out by Murdock and Phelps (1973). This involves an investigation of the musical tastes of school pupils. The sophistication with which this can be done depends upon the classroom group in question. Here we will

give some ideas, first for an 'A' level sociology group and then
for a group of 'non-academic' early leavers.

Since Murdock and Phelps themselves use a range of methods
from questionnaires to unstructured interviews, the first point
for discussion might be the pros and cons of the various method-
ologies. Pupils might try both approaches and compare the results.
Once pupils try and formulate their own questionnaires they will
soon recognise some of the limitations of the Murdock and Phelps
one. They are also likely to question the wisdom of measuring
pupils' 'pop involvement' simply on pupils' knowledge of the current Top Twenty singles records. Special attention can be paid
to the problems of formulating totally unambiguous questions.
For example, even a question that Murdock and Phelps regarded
as totally straightforward - namely, 'How often do you buy a pop
record?' - is likely to be interpreted in very different ways by
various pupils. Many pupils would never dream of referring to
their 'progressive' rock records as merely 'pop'.

Another key issue will be sampling. Pupils will need to think
about which characteristics of pupils are most likely to affect their
musical tastes (e.g. their sex, their age, their academic level,
identification with any particular youth styles etc.) and ensure
that the questionnaire is suitably sampled to each of these groups.

A 'non-academic' group will obviously not have the background
knowledge to deal with the more theoretical issues of methodology,
questionnaire design and sampling. However, they would be quite
capable of carrying out a more limited questionnaire survey.
Corrigan (1979), for example, compares the musical tastes of two
working-class comprehensive schools in Sunderland by simply
asking pupils to list their five favourite pop stars/groups. Carried
out in 1970, he uncovered some interesting differences which
suggest that the clear patterning of choice by social class reported
in Murdock and Phelps (1973) might be misleading. Despite the
fact that there were no obvious differences in the two Sunderland
schools, the pupils' tastes in one were dominated by hard rock
groups like Deep Purple and Led Zeppelin, whilst in the other
more traditional pop singers were highly rated (Tom Jones appeared
second on the list).

The other dimension to Murdock and Phelps's research - that
of unstructured interviewing - is particularly suitable as a research tool for more 'non-academic' pupils. All this requires is
sensitive discussion with either individuals or groups of pupils
concerning their musical likes and dislikes. These interviews
might be tape recorded, especially if the pupils doing them are
disinclined (or even unable) to take written notes while interviewing.

Any investigations by pupils are likely to serve as a very useful basis for discussion in the classroom. Pupils can be asked how
many different youth styles they can remember and when they
occurred? What did these groups look like? What kind of music
did they listen to? Why do these groups express themselves in
these particular ways? What kinds of reaction do they get from
the media, the police, the parents and teachers?

The teacher could put a subcultural 'map' on the blackboard -
a chart describing the dress, musical tastes, ritual activities etc.
of each subcultural style since the war (such as the teds, mods,
rockers, skinheads, hippies, glitter rockers, Northern soul
freaks, heavy metal rockers, punks etc.) Pupils always enjoy
filling in the spaces, and their memory of the small details of subcultural style is often amazing. Pupils could also interview relatives
such as older brothers and sisters, or even mothers and fathers)
about their involvement in any post-war youth cultures to get
some idea of former styles. Any tape recordings of interviews, or
photographic and journalistic evidence of post-war youth cultures,
could be stored in a central file as a resource for the whole class.
There is great scope here for English and drama teaching also.
Pupils can be encouraged to write personal accounts of their own
involvement in subcultures or of their reactions to others so involved. A play could be produced around the idea of youth culture
since the Second World War (for example, a group of pupils in
Stratford, East London produced such a play based on how the
meaning of 'being sixteen' in the area had changed over the past
fifty years).
A controversial, but potentially very fruitful, theme in those
areas with large immigrant communities might be to chart the different positions taken up by white youth cultures in relation to
the black presence. This could incorporate some of the following:
the teds' involvement in the Notting Hill race riots of 1956; the
mods emulating black styles, listening to soul and ska; skinheads
victimising Asians and yet copying black rude boys and dancing
to rocksteady and reggae (Fowler's essay Skins Rule in Gillett
(1972), would make excellent background reading for this); glitter
rockers turning away from black music altogether and developing
their own aesthetic; punks positively endorsing certain forms of
reggae and their involvement with the 'Rock Against Racism' campaign. In this respect, Dick Hebdige's book 'Reggae' would be
particularly helpful to pupils as it charts the relationship between
reggae and white youth culture, so revealing the often hidden
connections between black and white subcultures generally. More
advanced pupils might be interested in another book by Hebdige
on this theme - 'Subculture: The Meaning of Style' (1979).

9 BLACK STUDIES

INTRODUCTION

A recent discussion paper Local Authorities and Multi-Cultural Education (published by the Labour Party's race relations action group) has argued that 'the school curriculum remains essentially ethnocentric with an implicit built-in assumption that white Western culture is superior.' It suggests that most schools fail to consider the positive achievements of black people and fail to introduce pupils to the major characteristics of black cultures. This view reinforces our central thesis concerning the importance of a cross-cultural perspective on music.

The serious study of contemporary popular music could go a long way to offset this bias. Three of the eight books in this series (GV, SF and DH) are specifically concerned with black music styles. Moreover, one of the principal themes of the series is that Afro-American music has been the major influence on much contemporary popular music. Graham Vulliamy's 'Jazz and Blues' traces the way in which a new musical tradition was born as the result of the merging of two other traditions - the African and the European - in the Southern states of America. John Shepherd's 'Tin Pan Alley' shows how the commercial white American popular music industry periodically created new markets by appropriating and diluting black American forms into white, adolescent fashions, whilst Dave Rogers's 'Rock'n'Roll' illustrates how black rhythm and blues was a key ingredient in 1950s' rock'n'roll. Other books in the series testify to the dominance of black musical values today - in disco music, as discussed in Simon Frith's 'Soul and Motown', and in contemporary rock music (see Dave Rogers's 'Rock Music'). Finally, Dick Hebdige's 'Reggae' traces the other major tradition of black popular music - that emanating from the West Indies and culminating in this country with the reggae of West Indian communities.

The study of black music can be virtually meaningless without a corresponding study of the social conditions of slavery and colonialism from which it emerged. Not only are the lyrics of many blues, soul and reggae songs concerned directly with the facts of oppression, exploitation and poverty, but the very form of the music has frequently acted as an implicit protest against and rejection of the colonial system. Rhythm holds its own subversive significance. The insurrectionary connotations of African percussion amongst the black slaves were regarded by the slave-owners and colonial authorities as so potent and dangerous that drumming was periodically banned throughout the Southern states of America and the Caribbean. This social significance of rhythm is widely recognised, but Wishart (1980b) has gone further in arguing that the melodic and harmonic structure of the twelve bar blues was a direct expression of the social conditions facing blacks in the Southern states of America at the end of the last century.

Both Graham Vulliamy's 'Jazz and Blues' and Dick Hebdige's 'Reggae' contain sections on the historical background to slavery in America and the West Indies respectively. Here we felt it would be most useful in the 'Teachers' Guide' to enlarge upon Dick Hebdige's account. We have biased our discussion towards the history of the Caribbean (as opposed to the Americas) for a number of reasons:

1 Slavery in the Americas has been far more comprehensively documented in the literature to date. Many books on blues, and even on jazz, contain accounts of the slavery period.
2 Information on the West Indies is more relevant to the needs of British teachers setting up Black Studies courses.
3 Of all black music styles, reggae seems to be the most pre-occupied with the issues of black history and racial identity.

SLAVERY IN THE WEST INDIES

Although the first West Indian slaves were the islands' original inhabitants - the Carib and Arawak Indians - African slaves were being imported as early as 1518. However, the slave-trade did not really get under way until the end of the seventeenth century, reaching a peak in the middle of the 1700s when the famous 'triangular' flow of goods which linked Britain to Africa and the New World was fully established.

The British possessions - Barbados, Trinidad and Tobago, Jamaica, St Kitts, Nevis, Anguilla, Antigua, Montserrat and Guyana - were won in a series of wars with Spain, France and Holland which span the three centuries of the slave-trade. To begin with, these islands were used as a dumping ground for prisoners of war, political prisoners, criminals and prostitutes.

Much of the manual labour was carried out by indentured servants. They worked as virtual slaves for the four to five years of their 'apprenticeship' and were then granted their freedom and a small plot of land. These white menials were likely, at this stage, to fare rather worse than the enslaved blacks who toiled alongside them. Slaves were relatively expensive (fetching between £25 and £30 in 1650) and were thus valuable assets to be carefully preserved, whereas indentured servants whose labour could only be guaranteed for a limited period of time were worked much harder.

The development of a plantation economy, producing sugar for the European market, led to the need for a larger and more disciplined workforce. Africa could supply such a force. Thus the

slave-trade, opened up originally by the Portuguese but later
dominated by the British, began in earnest. Two companies - the
Royal Adventurers Trading to Africa and the Royal Africa Company
- were granted charters in 1660 and 1672. They were concerned
exclusively with the transport of human cargo from Africa to the
New World. Between 1627 and 1775 some 1,500,000 slaves were
imported into the British West Indies and the same number were
carried to other colonies. But these figures do not give an accurate
indication of the size of the slave-trade because many slaves went
unrecorded and many more perished before they even reached
the West Indies.

Thousands of Africans died on the plantations during the period
of acclimatisation (which was called the 'seasoning' in the slave-
owners' jargon) from a variety of illnesses which ranged from
dysentry and smallpox to lockjaw and 'despondency' - in simple
language, the loss of the will to live. Thousands, perhaps millions
more perished at sea during the notorious Middle Passage - the
gruelling voyage from Africa to the Caribbean. As much as fifty
per cent of the 'cargo' could be lost through fever, flux and the
occasional suicide. A vivid personal account of slavery is to be
found in the memoirs of Olaudah Equiano, a slave who bought his
freedom in 1766 and published his life story in 1789.

CULTURES OF RESISTANCE

Slaves did resist, despite the harsh regime of plantation work and
life under the slave codes. The Rastafarian movement, in its rejection of European values and its affirmation of the African roots
of black experience, is merely the most recent in a long line of
cultures which have resisted white domination in the Caribbean.

The earliest example of a significant uprising in the British
West Indies occurred in 1690 in Jamaica when some rebels, including a Coromantee boy called Cujo escaped to the hills after a slave
revolt in Chapelton. Cujo eventually established a 'maroon' (i.e.
'runaway slave' from the French 'maron') community. The maroons
under Cujo's leadership held out against the British soldiers for
almost fifty years until, on 1 March 1739, a treaty was signed
ending the war. One of the treaty's clauses stipulated that the
maroons who were now officially 'freemen' would 'kill, suppress or
destroy' all black rebels and return all future runaways.

There were revolts in all the British possessions in the West
Indies throughout the period of slavery. But it was on Saint-
Dominique in the French West Indies that the first successful black
revolution took place. Under the generalship of the mulatto states-
man, Toussaint L'Ouverture (and after the latter's capture, under
the black soldier Jean-Jacques Desselines), the black rebel forces
drove out the French in 1803. On 1 January 1804 Saint-Dominique
became Haiti - the world's first independent black republic. The
last large slave revolt in the British West Indies occurred in
Jamaica in 1831 when thousands of slaves, convinced that the auth-

orities were withholding their freedom papers, rose up and set
fire to many estates. After a minor victory against the local
militia, the rebels were hounded down by British forces and the
leader of the revolt, the Baptist minister Sam Sharpe, was hanged
in 1832. This rising probably accelerated the passage of the
Abolition Bill through the British House of Commons and slavery
was finally outlawed in 1834.

However, in 1865 hundreds of Jamaica's ex-slaves rose up, this
time demanding total self-government for the island's black population. Partly because of this rebellion, Jamaica became after 1865
even more firmly tied to Britain as a crown colony until, in 1938,
widespread discontent led to a series of strikes against low pay
and high unemployment. Ten strikers were killed and scores were
arrested in the subsequent clashes but the two major political
parties - the Jamaica Labour Party (JLP) and the People's
National Party (PNP) - grew out of the trades union movement
which had emerged during these years. Largely because of the
pressure applied by the JLP, led by Alexander Bustamante, and
the PNP, headed by Norman Manley (father of the present Prime
Minister, Michael), the whole adult male population was given the
vote for the first time in 1944. Jamaica finally achieved indepen-
dence in 1962 and Bustamante became the country's first prime
minister.

Sugar is still produced in the West Indies but it no longer
dominates the Caribbean economy. Instead, bauxite, tourism and
reggae earn Jamaica far more foreign money than the cultivation
of the sugar cane. The plantation system based on the cultivation
of a single crop and the naked exploitation of a large sub-class
of manual fieldhands no longer operates in its pure form. In fact,
Jamaica's PNP government has recently reorganised the sugar
industry and it is now run on co-operative lines with workers
participating in profit-sharing schemes.

Slavery days might seem a part of the Caribbean's distant past
now, but it is important to stress that the old plantation economy
has left its mark on the social and economic structures of present-
day Jamaica. The island is broadly divided into three classes
which still tend to correspond to the major racial groupings. The
people at the top, in the administration and in commerce, still
tend to be light-skinned Afro-Europeans - the products of inter-
marriage. The middle-class - small businessmen, shopkeepers,
bank managers and minor civil servants - are usually coloured,
Chinese, Syrian or Anglo-Indian (these last descended from indentured labourers brought to the island in the nineteenth century). And at the bottom we find that those in manual jobs or
unemployed are generally the black descendants of the West African
slaves. Unemployment is a real problem - seasonal joblessness on
the land can run as high as sixty per cent, and in 1972 Michael
Manley admitted in an interview for the BBC that between fifteen
and twenty per cent of Kingston's adult male population and at
least thirty per cent of the youth were unemployed.

CONCLUSION

There is little doubt that much of the wealth that Britain has enjoyed for the past 300 years was originally based on slavery and that the foundations of the considerable social and economic problems now facing the West Indies were laid in the 'glorious days' of the British Empire. These connections were recognised by those slaves who throughout the centuries resisted the rule of the white 'mas' and fought against a system they knew to be racist, exploitative and unjust. They confronted that system head-on with guns and axes, stones and homemade spears. But there were other less direct ways in which the slaves and their descendants could fight back. Music was one of the means through which they could express their resentment, anger and frustration. This is vividly brought out by the crucial episode in Dick Hebdige's 'Reggae' (taken from Alex Haley's 'Roots'), in which the enslaved Kunte Kinte and his companions were obliged to dance for the white sailors. The episode typifies the ambiguous nature of much black music; an outwardly light-hearted performance is shown to mask a bitter hostility.

The preservation of key aspects of West African musical traditions testifies to that legacy of underground resistance to white domination. Thus, at any point in the history of the music, the combination of black and white musical styles begins to take on a slightly different significance if the experiences of slavery and colonialism are foregrounded. The lyrical content of much contemporary reggae (Rastafarianism, Back to Africa etc.) merely mirrors themes which are embodied at the level of form in the rhythmic structure of the music. And reggae is just one example, though an extreme one, of the tradition of resistance in black music. There is a similar concern with the African heritage and with issues of social and racial inequality in much modern jazz and free jazz and in much soul music. Unless we can refer some of the tension and discord in black music back to the roots of the black experience in slavery, much of the music's significance - and its power and appeal for black people - will be lost.

SUGGESTIONS FOR FURTHER READING

Slavery

The following would be suitable texts on this theme for pupils:

Agnet, I., 'A Pictorial History of the Slave Trade', Minerva, 1971. A useful anthology of prints and photographs.
Howard, R., 'Black Cargo', Documentary History Series, Wayland, 1972.
Mountfield, A., 'The Slave Trade', Wayland, 1973. These last two books provide a straightforward and well-illustrated history of the slave trade.

Langdon-Davis, J. (ed.), 'The Slave Trade and its Abolition',
Jackdaw Publications no. 12. A compilation of documents in a
loose folder. Available from Jackdaw Publications, 30 Bedford
Square, London, W.C.1.
Lester, J., 'To Be a Slave', Longman Young, 1970. A collection
of short pieces of writing by American slaves. Used in conjunction with a collection of country blues recordings, this
could serve as a source book for anyone interested in teaching about conditions on the plantations in the United States.

There are two drawbacks to using the above-mentioned texts
with young black students. First, those books which deal with the
slave-trade tend to explain abolition solely in terms of Wilberforce
and pressure from the Abolitionist Movement in England. This
ignores other factors such as the decline of the sugar industry,
the impact of the French Revolution, and the efforts of the slaves
themselves to make the system unworkable. The second more
general problem is that many black rasta-influenced pupils may
refuse to respond to images of enslaved blacks on the grounds
that such imagery demeans their race. One teaching strategy here
might be to move directly on to the Caribbean material and to
focus on the slaves' own cultures of resistance.
Teachers will find the following three books to be full and
detailed accounts of slavery in the West Indies and all containing
historical documentary material:

Craton, M., Walvin, J. and Wright D., 'Slavery, Abolition and
Emancipation', Longman, 1976.
Dunn, R., 'Sugar and Slaves: The Rise of the Planter Class in
the English West Indies (1624-1713)', Cape, 1973.
Sheridan, R., 'Sugar and Slavery', Caribbean Universities
Press, 1974.
Olaudah Equiano's narrative can be found in:
Curtin, P. (ed), 'Africa Remembered: Narratives by West
Africans', University of Wisconsin Press, 1967.

A book that makes essential reading for anyone interested in
tracing back the roots of blues and jazz to American slave culture
is Eugene Genovese's 'Roll, Jordan, Roll' (Deutsch, 1975). The
book is extremely detailed and thorough and concentrates on the
lived experience of slavery in the cotton plantations of the South
and recounts the story of the formation of a distinct slave culture
in America.
Finally, Alex Haley's 'Roots' (Picador, 1979) provides a vivid,
fictional account of a West African slave's transportation to the
New World and follows the fortunes of both himself and his descendants in America.

Cultures of Resistance

Leonard Barrett's 'The Rastafarians: Dreadlocks of Jamaica' (Heinemann, 1977) contains a comprehensive, but fairly condensed, chapter on the various insurrections and radical movements that preceded Rastafarianism in Jamaica. See also the chapter on the maroons in 'Reggae Bloodlines' by Stephen Davis and Peter Simon (Anchor, 1977), whilst 'The Fighting Maroons of Jamaica' by Carey Robinson (Collins & Sangster, 1969) is the definitive history, but probably too narrowly focused for teachers only generally interested in the Jamaican tradition of resistance. See Sheridan's 'Sugar and Slavery' for resistance on the other British possessions in the Caribbean.

For a more general introduction to and analysis of Jamaica's protest tradition see:

Boot, A. and Thomas, M., 'Jamaica: Babylon on a Thin Wire', Thames & Hudson, 1976.
Kuper, A., 'Changing Jamaica' Routledge & Kegan Paul, 1976. A sober, well-argued analysis of social conditions in contemporary Jamaica under the Manley regime.
Nettleford, R., 'Mirror, Mirror: Identity, Race and Protest in Jamaica', Morrow, 1972.

Black people in Britain

Hall, S., Jefferson, T., Clarke, J. and Roberts, B. 'Policing the Crisis', Macmillan, 1978. A scholarly account of the panic equating muggers with blacks which did so much to fuel British racism during the mid to late 1970s. Some good material on black identity.
John, G. and Humphrey, D., 'Because They're Black', Penguin, 1971. An anecdotal, qualitative study of racial discrimination in Britain.
Plummer, J., 'Movement of Jah People', Press Gang, 1978. A study of the Rastafarian movement, but the emphasis is on the significance of the cult for black British youth.
The Political and Economic Planning Report, 'Racial Discrimination in Britain', Penguin, 1976. A good source of facts and figures on this theme.
Pryce, K., 'Endless Pressure', Penguin, 1979. A cameo study of a relatively small West Indian community in Bristol. It is especially good on the significance of reggae and the sound systems for unemployed, black youth.
Stewart, P., 'Immigrants', Batsford, 1976. A useful introduction to the theme aimed at pupils.
'Talking Blues' (AFFOR). A small book containing a series of transcribed interviews with black youths in Handsworth, Birmingham. Black-police relations is a major theme.

SOME TEACHING SUGGESTIONS

A project on roots

Ask pupils to present a historical reconstruction of the passage
of African peoples through the Caribbean and on to America and
Britain and to compile dates, statistics, facts and personal
accounts of each stage of the journey. How were slaves transported
and in what numbers from which tribes over how long a period of
time? What were the patterns of immigration from the West Indies
into Britain and the United States in the period after the Second
World War? How and where did the immigrants settle? What kinds
of jobs did they do? Ask pupils to search for reggae records
which deal with this passage (e.g. 'Slavery Days' by Burning
Spear, or 'Exodus' by Bob Marley). An exhibition of charts, maps
and readings could be mounted, and examples of African, Rastafarian and reggae music could be played.

Pupils could interview parents, neighbours etc. about the
experience of emigration and immigration, with a view to compiling
a set of recollections of the Caribbean. Tape recordings would be
ideal here, but if not then pupils should be asked to take as many
accurate notes as possible. What kind of place is the West Indies?
What does it look, taste, smell and sound like? What are conditions
like (housing, schools, quality of life)? What features of West
Indian life do they either miss or are glad to be rid of? In addition,
pupils should be encouraged to cut out from magazines as much
information as possible about life in the West Indies. They could
then compile a factual and visual dossier on the Caribbean (e.g.
travel articles, music advertisements, reggae articles, investigative
journalism etc.). The beginning of Dick Hebdige's book 'Reggae'
would give a useful theoretical framework within which to sift
this data - the difference between the 'two Jamaicas', with Rastas
and rude boys on the one hand and beaches and tourists on the
other.

A project on the Rastafarian contribution to reggae

Pupils should cut out and collect as much information as possible
on the Rastafarian cult. Collages could be assembled and charts
drawn up listing the central tenets, beliefs and taboos of the
movement. Record sleeves celebrating Rastafarian rituals, dress
and hairstyles could be collected and examples of Rasta art (re)-
produced (e.g. Ras Daniel Heartman's dreadlock portraits). A
poetry reading could be included - examples of Rasta poetry can
be found in L. E. Barrett's book 'The Rastafarians', on record
sleeves and in black magazines. Linton Kwesi Johnson's work,
though not directly Rastafarian, could be included here and would
provide the perfect hinge between music and literature for a black
studies course in British schools. His 'Dread, Beat and Blood' is
available in book form (Bogle l'Ouverture, 1979) and on record

(Virgin, 1978). Pupils should be encouraged to write their own soul, reggae or jazz poems using the rhythms of the various musical styles to blend with - or cut across - the messages they are trying to convey. Spencer (1981a) describes how teachers can capitalise upon the remarkable facility of many West Indian pupils for toasting (improvised commentary). Teachers are reminded that in projects of this sort, or in the kinds of interviews suggested earlier, the speakers may choose to use West Indian forms of English. These are variously referred to as dialect, patois or creole. The work of Edwards (1979) and others indicate ways of making a positive approach to these non-standard forms of English. There are also possibilities here for drama. Pupils could produce a short, dramatic reconstruction of the history of the Rastas from slavery to exile and ignominy to a kind of acceptance as the spokesmen of black, West Indian experience - as the representatives of a truly Jamaican culture.

The American experience

Where Dick Hebdige's 'Reggae' would provide much of the material for the above two projects, Graham Vulliamy's 'Jazz and Blues' and Simon Frith's 'Soul and Motown' focus upon the black experience in the United States. A useful project here is to ask pupils to use the lyrics of blues and soul numbers to chart the changing position of blacks in American society. Two books are particularly useful in this respect:

Oliver, P., 'The Meaning of the Blues', Collier Books, 1963.
Haralambos, M., 'Right On: From Blues to Soul in Black America',
     Eddison Press, 1974.

Black music and literature could also be linked in a study of black people in the United States. Of special relevance here would be extracts from James Baldwin's novels, from 'The Autobiography of Malcolm X' (Penguin, 1970) and from Eldridge Cleaver's 'Soul on Ice' (Panther, 1970).
    Finally, teachers might introduce pupils who are music specialists to studies of the nature of the African influence on Afro-American music. Key texts here would include:

Oliver, P., 'Savannah Syncopators - African Retentions in the
     Blues', November Books, 1970.
Roberts, J.S., 'Black Music of Two Worlds', Allen Lane, 1972.
Schuller, G., 'Early Jazz', Chapter 1, Oxford University Press,
     1968.
Wishart, T., The Blues: An Ideal-Typical Example, in
     Shepherd, J., Virden, P., Vulliamy, G. and Wishart, T. 'Whose
     Music? A Sociology of Musical Languages', pp. 166-77,
     Transaction Books, 1980.

10 REFERENCES

Abrams, M. (1959), 'The Teenage Consumer', London Press
   Exchange Ltd.
Andrews, H.K. (1958), 'An Introduction to the Technique of
   Palestrina', Novello.
Bebey, F. (1975), 'African Music: A People's Art', Harrap.
Belz, C. (1973), 'The Story of Rock', Harper & Row.
Bourdieu, P. (1971), Intellectual Field and Creative Project, re-
   printed in Young, M.F.D. (ed.) (1971).
Burnett, M. (1981), Teaching pop to the Middle Age Range, in
   Vulliamy, G. and Lee, E. (1981).
Cashdan, A. et al. (1974), 'Language in Education', Open Univer-
   sity Press.
Chester, A. (1970), Second Thoughts on a Rock Aesthetic: The
   Band, 'New Left Review', 62.
Cobbson, F. (1981), African Drumming, in Vulliamy, G. and Lee,
   E. (1981).
Cohen, S. (1973), 'Folk Devils and Moral Panics', Paladin.
Coleman, A. (1961), 'The Adolescent Society', Free Press.
Collinson, F. (1966), 'The Traditional and National Music of
   Scotland', Routledge & Kegan Paul.
Comer, J. (1981a), How Can I Use the Top Ten?, in Vulliamy, G.
   and Lee, E. (1981).
Comer, J. (1981b), Rhythm and Percussion Work in Afro-American
   Styles, in Vulliamy, G. and Lee, E. (1981).
Cooke, D. (1955), 'The Language of Music', Oxford University
   Press.
Corrigan, P. (1979), 'Schooling the Smash Street Kids', Macmillan.
Daniélou, A. (1968), 'Ragas of Northern Indian Music', Barrie.
DeWitt, J. (1976), 'Rhythmic Figures for Bassists', vol. 2, Hansen.
Dwyer, T. (1975), 'Making Electronic Music', Oxford University
   Press.
Edwards, V. (1979), 'The West Indian Language Issue in British
   Schools', Routledge & Kegan Paul.
Eliot, T.S. (1948), 'Notes Towards the Definition of Culture',
   Faber & Faber.
Farmer, P. (1981), Examining Pop, in Vulliamy, G. and Lee, E.
   (1981).
Fisher, G. (1981), Teaching West Indian Steel Band Music, in
   Vulliamy, G. and Lee, E. (1981).
Floyd, L. (1981), A Glimpse of Indian Music, in Vulliamy, G. and
   Lee, E. (1981).
Frith, S. (1978), 'The Sociology of Rock', Constable.

Gillett, C. (ed.) (1972), 'Rock File', Penguin.

Green Note Music (1973), 'Improvising Rock Guitar'.

Gutcheon, J. (1978), 'Improvising Rock Piano', Consolidated Music Publishers.

Hall, S., Jefferson, T. and Clarke, J. (eds) (1976), 'Resistance through Rituals', Hutchinson.

Hammick, V. (1975), 'Electric Bass Technique', Gwyn Publishing.

Harvey, E. (1975), 'Teach Yourself Jazz Piano', English Universities Press.

Hebdige, D. (1979), 'Subculture: The Meaning of Style', Methuen.

Hodeir, A. (1956), 'Jazz: Its Evolution and Essence', Secker & Warburg.

Jefferson, T. (1976), Cultural Responses of the Teds, in Hall, S. et al. (1976).

Jones, A.M. (1959), 'Studies in African Music', Oxford University Press.

Karpeles, M. (1973), 'An Introduction to English Folk Song', Oxford University Press.

Kaye, C. (1969-71), 'How to Play the Electric Bass' (4 vols), Ashley Fields.

Keil, C. (1966a), Motion and Feeling through Music, 'Journal of Aesthetics and Art Criticism', 24.

Keil, C. (1966b), 'Urban Blues', University of Chicago Press.

Kerper, M. (1977), 'Jazz Riffs for Piano', Amsco.

King, B.B. (1973), 'Blues Guitar', Charles Hansen.

Labov, W. (1974), The Logic of Non-Standard English, in Cashdan, A. et al. (1974).

Latin Percussion Ltd (1974), 'Understanding Latin Rhythms', handbook to LP of the same title, P LPV 337.

Leavis, F. (1943), 'Education and the University', Chatto & Windus.

Lee, E. (1970), 'Music of the People', Barrie & Jenkins.

Lee, E. (1972), 'Jazz: An Introduction', Stanmore Press.

Lee, E. (1976a), A Note on Conventions of Notation in Afro-American Music, in Vulliamy, G. and Lee, E. (1976).

Lee, E. (1976b), Pop and the Teacher: Some Uses and Problems, in Vulliamy, G. and Lee, E. (1976).

Lee, E. (1981a), Bringing the Guitar into Your School, in Vulliamy, G. and Lee, E. (1981).

Lee, E. (1981b), The Foremost Medium: The Voice, in Vulliamy, G. and Lee, E. (1981).

Lomax, A. (1968), 'Folk Song Style and Culture', Transaction Books.

Mellers, W. (1973), 'Twilight of the Gods: The Beatles in Retrospect', Faber & Faber.

Meyer, L.B. (1956), 'Emotion and Meaning in Music', Chicago University Press.

Meyer, L.B. (1959), Some Remarks on Value and Greatness in Music, 'Journal of Aesthetics and Art Criticism', 1.

Morales, H. (1949), 'Latin-American Instruments and How to Play Them', Kar-Val Publishing.

Mungham, G. and Pearson, G. (eds) (1976), 'Working Class Youth

Culture', Routledge & Kegan Paul.
Murdock, G. and Phelps, G. (1973), 'Mass Media and the Secondary School', Macmillan.
Neville, R. (1971), 'Playpower', Paladin.
Nicholls, M. (1976), Running an 'Open' Music Department, in Vulliamy, G. and Lee, E. (1976).
Nketia, J.H.K. (1975), 'The Music of Africa', Gollancz.
Paynter, J. and Aston, A. (1970), 'Sound and Silence', Cambridge University Press.
Reich, C. (1972), 'The Greening of America', Penguin.
Robins, T. (1976), The Presentation of Pop Music, in Vulliamy,G. and Lee, E. (1976).
Rogers, D. (1976), Varieties of Pop Music: a Guided Tour, in Vulliamy, G. and Lee, E. (1976).
Schuller, G. (1968), 'Early Jazz', Oxford University Press.
Sharp, C. (1965), 'English Folk Song: Some Conclusions': Mercury Books.
Shepherd, J., Virden, P., Vulliamy, G. and Wishart, T. (1980), 'Whose Music? A Sociology of Musical Languages', Transaction Books.
Shepherd, J. (1980) Chapters 1-3 of Shepherd, J. et al. 1980a.
Sims, L. (1928), 'Piano Method (Jazz)', Keith Prowse.
Spencer, P. (1976a), The Blues: a Practical Project for the Classroom, in Vulliamy, G. and Lee, E. (1976).
Spencer, P. (1976b), The Creative Possibilities of Pop, in Vulliamy, G. and Lee, E. (1976). This work is illustrated on an accompanying cassette, 'Pop Music in School: Illustrations'.
Spencer, P. (1981a), Vocal Improvisation, in Vulliamy, G. and Lee, E. (1981).
Spencer, P. (1981b), Reggae, in Vulliamy, G. and Lee, E. (1981).
Titon, J.T. (1977), 'Early Downhome Blues', University of Illinois Press.
Ulehla, L. (1966), 'Contemporary Harmony', Free Press.
Vulliamy, G. (1976a), Definitions of Serious Music, in Vulliamy, G. and Lee, E. (1976).
Vulliamy, G. (1976b), Pupil-Centred Music Teaching, in Vulliamy, G. and Lee, E. (1976).
Vulliamy, G. (1980a), Music and the Mass Culture Debate, in Shepherd, J. et al. (1980).
Vulliamy, G. (1980b), Music as a Case Study in the New Sociology of Education, in Shepherd, J. et al. (1980).
Vulliamy, G. and Lee, E. (1976), 'Pop Music in School', Cambridge University Press. Second (revised) edn 1980.
Vulliamy, G. and Lee, E. (1981), 'Pop, Rock and Ethnic Music in School', Cambridge University Press.
Wilder, A. (1972), 'American Popular Song: The Great Innovators 1900-1950', Oxford University Press.
Willis, P. (1978), 'Profane Culture', Routledge & Kegan Paul.
Wishart, T. (1974), 'Sounds Fun', Schools Council.
Wishart, T. (1980a), Musical Writing, Musical Speaking, in Shepherd, J. et al. (1980).

Wishart, T. (1980b), The Blues: An Ideal-Typical Example, in
  Shepherd, J. et al. (1980), pp. 166–77.
Young, M.F.D. (ed.) (1971), 'Knowledge and Control: New
  Directions for the Sociology of Education', Collier Macmillan.

SECTION III
Further resources

INTRODUCTION

We have so far given a theoretical justification for our series (section I) and a summary of the cognitive framework of some major topics, together with suggestions for classroom use (section II). However, a teacher who wishes to undertake courses in popular music needs a body of further resources as back-up material, and to enhance his own knowledge. Section III aims to meet this need. We have kept this relatively brief both for reasons of space and because we felt that priority should be given to providing a sound theoretical framework. Furthermore, a very extensive, and guided, bibliography and discography is given in 'Pop Music in School' (Cambridge University Press, revised edn, 1980).

This section III is presented book by book. There is a slight difference in format from subject to subject, as we allowed each contributor to present his suggestions in the way which he felt would be most suitable. To avoid duplication, authors have not listed books or records already included in the Suggestions for Reading and Listening at the end of each of the pupils' books.

11 'FOLKSONG AND MUSIC HALL'
by Edward Lee

BIBLIOGRAPHY

Folk music

General information
English Folk Dance and Song Society (EFDSS), Cecil Sharp House,
2 Regent's Park Road, London NW1 7AY. Telephone: (01-) 485-
2206. This has a unique library. A wide selection of specialist
books can be obtained from the Folk Shop at the above address –
send s.a.e. for leaflets and catalogues.

Folk music and the teacher
Leach, R. and Palmer, R. (eds), 'Folk Music in School', Cambridge
University Press, 1978.

General books on English folk music
Karpeles, M., 'An Introduction to English Folk Song', Oxford
University Press, 1973.
Lloyd, A.L., 'Folk Song in England', Lawrence & Wishart, 1967.
Paperback edn, Paladin, 1975.

Social background
MacKerness, E.D., 'A Social History of English Music', Routledge
& Kegan Paul, 1964.

Folklore and customs
EFDSS (address above), leaflets available (note especially no. 1,
'May Day'; no. 5, 'Robin Hood'). These give a clear account of
the subject and a detailed source list.
Hole, C., 'A Dictionary of British Folk Customs', Paladin, 1978.

Anthologies of songs
Kennedy, P. (ed.), 'Folksongs of Great Britain and Ireland',
Cassell, 1975. Lists 360 songs, including lyrics in Celtic
languages.
Sedley, S., 'The Seeds of Love', Essex, 1967.
Silverman, J., 'The Folk Song Encyclopaedia', Chappell, 1975.
Contains 1000 songs.
Vaughan Williams, R. and Lloyd, A.L., 'The Penguin Book of
English Folk Song', Penguin, 1959.

Ballads
Child, F.J., 'The English and Scottish Popular Ballads' (5 vols),
  Houghton-Miffin, 1882-98. Reprinted by Dover Publications,
  1965.

Particular topics
Copper, B., 'A Song for Every Season', Paladin, 1975.
MacColl, E., 'The Shuttle and the Cage', Workers' Music Associ-
  ation, 1954.
Palmer, R., 'The Painful Plough', Cambridge University Press,
  1973.
Palmer, R., 'Poverty Knock', Cambridge University Press, 1974.
Palmer, R., 'The Valiant Sailor', Cambridge University Press,
  1973.
Raven, J., 'Victorian Inferno', Broadside, 1978.

Folk instruments and performance
Gould, T., 'Folk Guitar Tutor', EFDSS, 1966.

Celtic music
Breathnach, B., 'Folk Music and Dances of Ireland', Talbot Press,
  1971.
Collinson, F., 'The Traditional and National Music of Scotland',
  Routledge & Kegan Paul, 1966.
Gwyn Williams, W.S., 'Welsh National Music and Dance', Curwen,
  1932, reprinted by Gwynn, Llangollen, 1971.

The best source of information on Welsh traditional music is 'Canu
Gwerin' (journal of the Welsh Folk Song Society), Department of
Folklore, Welsh Folk Museum, St Fagan's, Cardiff CF5 6XB.

Folk music in the United States
Lomax, A., 'The Penguin Book of American Folk Songs', Penguin,
  1964.

For further suggestions see the notes by Brian Carroll, pp. 119-22.

Nineteenth-century music

General
Pearsall, R., 'Victorian Popular Music', David & Charles, 1973.
Pearsall, R., 'Edwardian Popular Music', David & Charles, 1975.

Street singers
Shephard, L., 'The History of Street Literature', David & Charles,
  1973.

Religious music
Temperley, N., 'The Music of the English Parish Church' (2 vols),
  Cambridge University Press, 1977.

Music of the middle classes
Fiske, R., 'English Theatre Music in the Eighteenth Century',
    Oxford University Press, 1973.
Jackson, R. (ed.), 'Stephen Foster Song Book', Dover, 1975.
Mander, R. and Mitchenson, J., 'Musical Comedy', Studio Vista,
    1969.
Southern, E., 'The Music of Black Americans', W.W. Norton, 1971.
    Includes work on minstrels.
A useful anthology of Stephen Foster's music entitled 'Immortal
Melodies', originally published by Robbins in 1939, is still available.

Music hall
Gammond, P., 'The Music Hall Songbook (1890-1920)', David &
    Charles, 1975.
Garrett, J.M., 'Sixty Years of British Music Hall', Chappell, 1976.
Hudd, R., 'Music Hall', Eyre Methuen, 1976. Profusely illustrated
    - excellent for classroom use.
Mander, R. and Mitchenson, J., 'British Music Hall', Studio Vista,
    1965.

Dancing

EFDSS, 'Folk and Country Dance' leaflet 4.
EFDSS, 'Morris Dance', leaflet 16.
Richardson, P.J.S., 'The Social Dances of the Nineteenth Cen-
    tury', Herbert Jenkins, 1960.
Wechsberg, J., 'The Waltz Emperors', Weidenfeld & Nicolson, 1973.

DISCOGRAPHY

Folk music

By far the most important British company concerned with the
issue of traditional folk recordings is Topic Records. Teachers
are thus advised to obtain one of their catalogues, either from
record shops, or directly from the company at Topic Records,
27 Nassington Road, London, NW3. Telephone: (01-) 435-9983.
Among the many records they have issued the following anthologies are typical:

    'The Child Ballads', 12T 160-1
    'The Valiant Sailor', 12TS 232 (see also, Palmer, R. in the
    particular topics section of the bibliography).
    'The Iron Muse', 12T 86
    'Steam Whistle Ballads', 12T 104

Celtic music is as yet not so well served, but the following records
produced by Tangent Records are worth a special mention:

'The Muckle Songs', TNGM 119
'Music from the Western Isles', TNGM 109

The nineteenth century

There is no specialist company as yet in this field, though some
records are issued by very small labels for specialist listeners.
For music which was popular from about 1890 to 1940, but which
was often written much earlier, the best source of information is
undoubtedly: The Vintage Light Music Society, 4 Harvest Bank
Road, West Wickham, Kent. The society issues a quarterly magazine at a very low cost, which concentrates on discographical
information, and on acting as a forum for interested persons. The
Secretary, Stuart Upton, is always willing to advise.
    Another source which teachers may find of use is: The British
Music Hall Society, 67 Russell Court, London WC1. The Secretary
is Mrs M. Sparks. The society holds monthly meetings and issues
a monthly magazine.
    Otherwise the main sources of music are the BBC, reissues, and
secondhand shops. The 'Radio Times' should be scanned regularly.
For example, recent programmes have dealt with the minstrel show,
George Formby and the work of Noel Coward. The big record companies are apt to delete at short notice, but seem willing to issue
a small amount of original material at a reasonable price, as well
as modern versions of old songs which vary in degree of authen-
ticity. Typical reissued originals in the shops at the time of writing are the anthologies 'On the Halls' (SHB 43) and 'Stars Who
Made the Music Hall' (ACL 1170).

12 'JAZZ AND BLUES'
by Graham Vulliamy

BOOKS

Background to Afro-American music

De Lerma, D.R. (ed.), 'Black Music in Our Culture', Kent State
University Press, 1970. A report of a symposium concerned
with the way in which black music could be incorporated into
the curricula of educational institutions in the United States.
Mellers, W., 'Music in a New Found Land', Barrie & Rockliff,
1964. A survey of twentieth-century American music. Part 2 is
largely devoted to Afro-American music.
Pleasants, H., 'Serious Music and all That Jazz', Gollancz, 1969.
A controversial and influential look by a classical music critic.
He argues that Afro-American music has provided the most
important musical development of this century.
Roberts, J.S., 'Black Music of Two Worlds', Allen Lane, 1973.
A history of Afro-American music, including the West Indian
traditions and the music of modern Africa.
Southern, E., 'The Music of Black Americans: A History', Norton,
1971.
Wilmer, V., 'The Face of Black Music', Da Capo Press, 1976.
A superb collection of photographs, together with quotes from
musicians. Introduction by saxophonist Archie Shepp.

Black culture in the United States

Genovese, E.D., 'Roll Jordan, Roll: The World the Slaves Made',
Andre Deutsch, 1975. A very detailed study of slave society
in the United States.
Levine, L.W., 'Black Culture and Black Consciousness: Afro-
American Folk Thought from Slavery to Freedom', Oxford University Press, 1977. An outstanding study of black American culture, including a lengthy chapter on black music.

Further reading on the blues

Albertson, C., 'Bessie: A Biography of Bessie Smith', Barrie &
Jenkins, 1973.
Broven, J., 'Walking to New Orleans', Blues Unlimited, 1974. The
story of post-war New Orleans rhythm and blues.

Charters, S., 'The Bluesmen', Oak Publications, 1967. Pre-war
rural blues.

Haralambos, M., 'Right On: From Blues to Soul in Black America',
Eddison Press, 1974. Relates the decline in popularity of blues
and increasing popularity of soul music among blacks to the
changing social and racial situation of black people in America.

Jones, Le Roi, 'Blues People', MacGibbon & Kee, 1965. A forceful
account by the black poet and playwright.

Keil, C., 'Urban Blues', Chicago University Press, 1966. Written
from a largely sociological viewpoint, featuring discussions of
B.B. King and Bobby Bland.

Leadbitter, M. and Napier, S. (eds), 'Nothing but the Blues',
Hanover Books, 1971. A collection of writings from 'Blues Unlimited Magazine'.

Middleton, R., 'Pop Music and the Blues', Gollancz, 1972. A sociological and musicological assessment of the relationships between
pop music and the blues.

Murray, A., 'Stomping the Blues', Quartet, 1978. A personal, and
sometimes controversial, view of the blues with a strong bias
towards jazz. Very well illustrated.

Rowe, M., 'Chicago Breakdown', Eddison Press, 1973. A study of
the blues in Chicago.

Titon, J., 'Early Downhome Blues: A Musical and Cultural Analysis', Illinois University Press, 1977. A very detailed musicological study of rural blues.

Mention should also be made of the excellent *Blues Paperbacks*
series, edited by Paul Oliver and published by Studio Vista Ltd.

Further reading on jazz

Berendt, J., 'The Story of Jazz', Barrie & Jenkins, 1978.
A collection of essays. Contains a very full discography and
the book is well illustrated.

Bethell, T., 'George Lewis: A Jazzman from New Orleans',
California University Press, 1978.

Collier, G., 'Jazz: A Student and Teacher's Guide', Cambridge
University Press, 1975. The first part of the book looks at the
history of jazz, while the second part deals with more practical
topics such as the teaching of jazz, composition, arrangement
and performance. A record of illustrations and a tape, which
can be used to provide backing for the practical exercises
suggested, are available separately.

Collier, J.L., 'The Making of Jazz: A Comprehensive History',
Granada Publishing, 1979.

Coryell, J. and Friedman, L., 'Jazz-Rock Fusion', Marion Boyars,
1978.

Cotterrell, R. (ed.), 'Jazz Now', Quartet, 1976. A collection of
articles, together with a reference section on British jazz, listing current performers, clubs, record labels, books and films.

Dankworth, A., 'Jazz: An Introduction to its Musical Basis',
  Oxford University Press, 1975.
Gammond, P., 'Scott Joplin and the Ragtime Era', Angus &
  Robertson, 1975.
Jewell, D., 'Duke: A Portrait of Duke Ellington', Sphere, 1978.
Kofsky, F., 'Black Nationalism and the Revolution in Music',
  Pathfinder Press, 1970. A discussion of the relationship between
  black avant-garde jazz in America and recent political and social
  movements among black people.
McCarthy, A., 'Big Band Jazz', Barrie & Jenkins, 1974.
Russell, R., 'Jazz Style in Kansas City and the South', California
  University Press, 1973.
Russell, R., 'Bird Lives!' Quartet, 1973. A superb biography of
  Charlie Parker.
Schuller, G., 'Early Jazz', Oxford University Press, 1968.
  A musical assessment of pre-Second World War jazz.
Spellman, A.B., 'Black Music: Four Lives', Schocken, 1970.
  Interesting profiles of four black American jazz musicians -
  Cecil Taylor, Ornette Coleman, Herbie Nichols and Jackie McLean.
Stearns, M., 'The Story of Jazz', Galaxy, 1971. A new edition of
  this useful history, first published in 1956.
Thomas, J.C., 'Chasin' the Trane: The Music and Mystique of
  John Coltrane', Elm Tree Books, 1976.
Williams, M., 'The Jazz Tradition', Oxford University Press, 1970.
Wilmer, V., 'As Serious as Your Life: The Story of the New Jazz',
  Quartet, 1977. A study of black avant-garde jazz, illustrated
  with some of the author's fine photographs.

For music teachers and students

Harvey, E., 'Teach Yourself Jazz Piano', English Universities
  Press, 1975.
Mehegan, J., 'Jazz Improvisation' (4 vols), Watson-Guptill, 1967.
Standifer, T.A. and Reeder, B., 'Source Book of African and
  Afro-American Materials for Music Educators', Contemporary
  Music Project, Music Educators National Conference, 1972.

There are a large number of instrumental tutors (particularly of
guitar) on the market, many of which are accompanied by a record
of musical examples. A well known publisher in this area is Green
Note Publications.

PERIODICALS

There are a number covering this area, some appearing rather
irregularly. 'Blues Unlimited Magazine' and 'Jazz Journal' are
particularly recommended.

RECORDS

The following book is a very helpful guide to the wide variety of records in this area, containing critical discussion of the records of leading jazz and blues artists:

McCarthy, A., Morgan, A., Oliver, P. and Harrison, M., 'Jazz on Record: A Critical Guide to the First 50 years, 1917-1967', Hanover Books (1968).

The two standard blues discographies are:

Godrich, J. and Dixon, R., 'Blues and Gospel Records 1902-1942', Storyville Publications, 1969.
Leadbitter, M. and Slaven, N., 'Blues Records 1943-1966', Hanover Books, 1968.

Since records are deleted and reissued at frequent intervals, I have only listed here a few LPs from some of the key performers mentioned in the book. Again, because of rapid changes, I have not given the numbers of the records, but simply the record label.

Armstrong, Louis, 'Memorial', double album, CBS.
Ayler, Albert, 'Spiritual Unity' ESP.
Bailey, Derek and Parker, Evans, 'The Topography of the Lungs', Incus.
Basie, Count, 'The Atomic Mr. Basie', Roulette.
Beiderbecke, Bix, 'Bix and his Gang', Parlophone.
Braxton, Anthony, 'The Complete Braxton', Freedom.
Broonzy, Big Bill, 'Big Bill Broonzy', Vogue.
Carr, Leroy and Blackwell, Scrapper, 'Blues before Sunrise', CBS.
Coleman, Ornette, 'Change of the Century', Atlantic.
Coltrane, John, 'Coltrane', Impulse.
Davis, Miles, 'In a Silent Way', CBS.
Ellington, Duke, 'Duke Ellington Meets Coleman Hawkins', Impulse.
Goodman, Benny, '1938 Cargegie Hall Jazz Concert', CBS.
Henderson, Fletcher, 'Fletcher Henderson and his Orchestra', vol. 1, RCA Victor.
Holliday, Billie, 'The Golden Years', vols 1 and 2, CBS.
Jackson, Mahalia, 'Mahalia', Columbia.
Jefferson, Blind Lemon, 'Penitentiary Blues', Riverside.
Johnson, Robert, 'King of the Delta Blues Singers', vol. 2, CBS.
Joplin, Scott, 'Ragtime Piano Roll Classics', BYG.
Jordan, Louis, 'The Best of Louis Jordan', MCA.
King, B.B., 'Live and Well', ABC.
Mingus, Charlie, 'Mingus Ah Um', Columbia.
Modern Jazz Quartet, 'European Concert', vols 1 and 2, Atlantic.
Monk, Thelonius, 'Brilliant Corners', Riverside.
Morton, Jelly Roll, 'King of New Orleans Jazz', vol. 1, RCA Victor.

Original Dixieland Jazz Band, 'Original Dixieland Jazz Band', RCA Victor.
Parker, Charlie (with Dizzy Gillespie), 'Bird and Diz', Saga.
Patton, Charley, 'Charley Patton', vol. 2, Origin.
Rushing, Jimmy, 'Jimmy Rushing Sings the Blues', Vanguard.
Shepp, Archie, 'Things Have Got To Change', Impulse.
Smith, Bessie, 'The World's Greatest Blues Singer', Columbia.
Taylor, Cecil, 'Silent Tongues', Arista Freedom.
Turner, Joe, 'The Boss of the Blues', Atlantic.
Walker, T Bone, 'T-Bone Blues', Atlantic.
Waters, Muddy, 'Muddy Waters at Newport', Chess.
Weather Report, 'Sweetnighter', Columbia.
Young, Lester, 'The Lester Young Story', vols 1 and 2 CBS.

13 'TIN PAN ALLEY'
by John Shepherd

Further resources for teaching this field are not, on the whole, difficult to find. A list of suitable texts is given below. The bibliography is divided into a number of sections: there is a reference section, a general section and then nine sections which follow chapters 2 to 10 of the book. There is no section for chapter 1, as background information to this chapter can quite adequately be found in the books listed in the general section. In all cases, the most recent date of publication is given.

REFERENCE

Jackson, Richard, 'United States Music: Sources of Bibliography and Collective Bibliography', Institute for Studies in American Music, City University of New York, 1973.
Kinkle, Roger E., 'The Complete Encyclopaedia of Popular Music and Jazz 1900-1950', Arlington House, 1974.
Rust, Brian, 'The American Dance Band Discography 1917-1942', Arlington House, 1975.

GENERAL

Ewen, David, 'All the Years of American Popular Music', Prentice-Hall, 1977.
Gelatt, Roland, 'The Fabulous Phonograph 1877-1977', Cassell, 1977.
Goldberg, Isaac, 'Tin Pan Alley', Frederick Ungar, 1961.
Spaeth, Sigmund, 'A History of Popular Music in America', Phoenix House, 1948.
Whitcomb, Ian, 'After the Ball', Penguin, 1972.
Whitcomb, Ian, 'Tin Pan Alley: A Pictorial History 1919-1939' Paddington Press, 1975.
Witmark, Isodore and Goldberg, Isaac, 'The Story of the House of Witmark', Lee Furman, 1939.

CHAPTER 2

Jackson, Richard, 'Popular Songs of Nineteenth-Century America', Dover Publications, 1976.
Roach, Hildred, 'Black American Music', Crescendo Publishing, 1973.

Sobel, Bernard, 'A Pictorial History of Vaudeville', Bonanza
   Books, 1961.
Southern, Eileen, 'The Music of Black Americans', W.W. Norton,
   1971.

CHAPTER 3

Blesh, Rudi and Janis, Harriet, 'They All Played Ragtime', Oak
   Publications, 1971.
Gammond, Peter, 'Scott Joplin and the Ragtime Era', Abacus, 1975.
Schafer, William J. and Riedel, Johannes, 'The Art of Ragtime',
   Louisiana State University Press, 1973.

CHAPTER 4

Franks, A.H., 'Social Dance: A Short History', Routledge & Kegan
   Paul, 1963.
Freedland, M., 'Irving Berlin', W.H. Allen, 1974.
Handy, W.C., 'Father of the Blues', Sidgwick & Jackson, 1961.
McCarthy, Albert, 'The Dance Band Era', Studio Vista, 1970.
McCarthy, Albert, 'Big Band Jazz', Barrie & Jenkins, 1974.

CHAPTER 5

Brunn, H.O., 'The Story of the Original Dixieland Jazz Band',
   Sidgwick & Jackson, 1961.
Leonard, Neil, 'Jazz and the White Americans', Chicago University
   Press, 1962.
Whiteman, Paul and McBride, Mary Margaret, 'Jazz', J.H. Sears,
   1926.

CHAPTER 6

Green, Stanley, 'The World of Musical Comedy', A.S. Barnes, 1960.
Green, Stanley, 'The Rodgers and Hammerstein Story', W.H.
   Allen, 1965.
Jablonski, Edward and Stewart, Lawrence D., 'The Gershwin
   Years', Robson Books, 1974.
Thomas, Tony and Terry, Jim, 'The Busby Berkely Book', Thames
   & Hudson, 1973.
Wilder, Alec, 'American Popular Song', Oxford University Press,
   1972.

CHAPTER 7

Goodman, Benny and Kolodin, Irving, 'The Kingdom of Swing',
   Ungar Publishing, 1961.

Green, Jonathan, 'Glenn Miller and the Age of Swing', Dempsey & Squires, 1976.
Sanford, Herb, 'Tommy and Jimmy: the Dorsey Years', Ian Allan, 1972.
Shaw, Artie, 'The Trouble with Cinderella', Farrar, Straus & Young, 1952.
Simon, George T., 'Glenn Miller and His Orchestra', W.H. Allen, 1974.
Simon, George T., 'The Big Bands', Collier, 1975.

CHAPTER 8

Anderton, Barrie, 'Sonny Boy: the World of Al Jolson', Jupiter, 1975.
Barnes, Ken, 'Sinatra and the Great Song Stylists', Ian Allan, 1972.
Crosby, Bing, 'Call Me Lucky', Frederick Muller, 1955.
Frank, Alan, 'Sinatra', Hamlyn Publishing, 1978.
Kahn, E.J., Jr, 'The Voice', Musicians Press, 1946.
Pleasants, Henry, 'The Great American Popular Singers', Victor Gollancz, 1974.
Scaduto, Tony, 'Frank Sinatra', Michael Joseph, 1976.
Thompson, Charles, 'Bing: the Authorised Biography', W.H. Allen, 1975.

CHAPTER 9

Lynn, Vera, 'Vocal Refrain', W.H. Allen, 1975.
Pearsall, Ronald, 'Popular Music of the 20's', David & Charles, 1976.
Randall, Alan and Seaton, Ray, 'George Formby', W.H. Allen, 1974.

CHAPTER 10

Jones, Peter, 'Tom Jones', Avon, 1971.

THE MUSIC

A list of recordings is not given here for two reasons. First, the text itself indicates which artists are the ones whose work should be sought out. Second, record companies change their catalogues very rapidly. However, big, city-centre record shops stock recordings made by musicians who worked in the Alley tradition from the early 1920s onwards, for example. Again, Hollywood musicals from the 1930s (the Astaire/Rogers and Busby Berkely films are the most famous of these) are quite frequently shown on the television, as are films starring the leading bands of the swing era. There are also a number of radio programmes which feature the different kinds of music referred to in Tin Pan Alley, as well as focus on the lives and careers of the more important and influential personalities. Finally, sheet music representative of the different styles of songs and dance band numbers discussed in the book can be found in most big music stores (Richard Jackson's 'Popular Songs of Nineteenth-Century America' contains most of the songs mentioned in chapter 2, for example). Volume 1 of Roger D. Kinkle's 'The Complete Encyclopaedia of Popular Music and Jazz' gives a year by year account of the most popular commercial songs, and will provide teachers with a good starting-point from which to identify music which is within their own experience.

14 'ROCK 'N' ROLL'
by Dave Rogers

INTO THE FIFTIES

Ray, Johnny, 'American Legend', CBS Embassy 31696.

Teddy boys

Bogdanor, V. and Skidelsky, R., 'The Age of Affluence 1951-
  1964', Macmillan, 1970.
Fyvel, T.R., 'The Insecure Offenders', Penguin, 1963.
Jefferson, Tony, Cultural Responses of the Teds: The Defence of
  Space and Status, in S. Hall and T. Jefferson (eds), 'Resistance
  Through Rituals', Hutchinson, 1976.

ROCK AROUND THE CLOCK

Bill Haley and His Comets, 'Rock The Joint!', Rollercoaster ROLL
  2002 (American hits prior to 'Shake Rattle and Roll').

COUNTRY MUSIC

Malone, Bill C., 'Country Music USA', Texas University Press,1967.
Monroe, Bill, 'Best of Bill Monroe', MCA MCF 2696.
Shestack, M., 'The Country Music Encyclopaedia', Omnibus Press.
Williams, R.M., 'Sing A Sad Song - The Life of Hank Williams',
  Ballantine Books, 1973.
Wills, Bob, 'The Bob Wills Anthology' CBS Embassy 31611.

RHYTHM 'N' BLUES

Fong-Torres, B. (ed.), Interview with Johnny Otis in 'The
  Rolling Stone Interviews, vol. 2', Warner Paperbacks, Straight
  Arrow Publishers, 1973 (particularly interesting).
Haralambos, Michael, 'Right On: From Blues to Soul in Black
  America', Eddison Press, 1973.
Jordan, L., 'The Best of Louis Jordan', MCA MCFM 2715.
Oliver, Paul, 'The Story Of the Blues', Barrie & Jenkins, 1978.
  Final chapters.

Turner, Joe, 'His Greatest Recordings', Atlantic K 40525.

GOOD ROCKIN' TONIGHT

Some of the earliest and most fascinating tapes made by Elvis at Sun in 1954-5 are on:

'The Best of Sun Rockabilly', vols 1 and 2, Charly CR 30123 and CR 30124.
'Good Rocking Tonight', Bopcat 100.
'Imperial Rockabillies', United Artists UAS 30101.
'Rare Rockabilly', MCA MCFM 2697.

HAIL HAIL ROCK'N'ROLL!

The Ace Story, vols 1 and 2, Ace/Chiswick CH 11 and CH 12.
Broven, J., 'Walking To New Orleans', Blues Unlimited, 1974.
  Together with 'The Ace Story' this makes up a good introduction to rhythm 'n' blues and rock 'n' roll from New Orleans.
Diddley, Bo, 'Golden Decade', Chess 6310 123.
Farren, M. (ed.), 'Elvis In His Own Words', Omnibus Press, 1976.
Finnis, Rob and Dunham, Bob, 'Gene Vincent and The Blue Caps' 1974. This is the definitive account of Vincent in the 1950s.
Groia, Phil, 'They All Sang On The Corner', Edmond Publishing, 1973.
Guralnick, P., 'Feel Like Going Home: Portraits in Blues and Rock 'n' Roll', Omnibus Press, 1978.
Lydon, M., 'Rock Folk', Dial Press 1971 (especially the essays by Lydon on Carl Perkins and Jerry Lee Lewis).
Lymon, Frankie and The Teenagers, 'Why Do Fools Fall In Love?', Pye NSPL 28251.
Millar, Bill, 'The Drifters: The Rise and Fall Of The Black Vocal Group', November Books, 1971. Both this and Phil Groia's book deal with doo-wop.
Presley, Elvis, '40 Greatest', RCA PL 42691.

ROCK ISLAND LINE

Dene, Terry, 'I Thought Terry Dene Was Dead', Decca SPA 368.
Melly, George, 'Owning Up', Penguin, 1970. A fascinating view of the impact of rock'n'roll when he was the singer with Mick Mulligan's jazz band.
Steele, Tommy, 'Focus On Tommy Steele', Decca FOS 21/2.
Wooding, Dan, 'I Thought Terry Dene Was Dead', Coverdale House, 1974.

BACK IN THE USA

Burnette, Johnny, 'Johnny Burnette and The Rock 'n' Roll Trio',
   MCA Coral CDLM 8054.
The Coasters, '20 Great Originals', Atlantic K 30057.
Eddy, Duane, 'Legend of Rock', London DLLW 5003/4.
The Everly Brothers, 'Don and Phil's Fabulous Fifties Treasury',
   Phonogram 6310 300.
Gillett, Charlie, 'Making Tracks: Atlantic Records and the Growth
   of a Multi-Million Dollar Industry', Panther, 1975.
Hawkins, Ronnie, 'Rockin' ', Pye NSPL 28238.
Jackson, Wanda, 'Rockin' With Wanda', Capitol CAPS 1007.
Millar, Bill, 'The Coasters', Star Books, 1975.
Nelson, Ricky, 'The Very Best Of Ricky Nelson', United Artists
   Sunset SLS 50164.
Wray, Link, 'There's Good Rockin' Tonite', Union Pacific UP 002.

THIS ROCK 'N' ROLL HAS GOT TO GO. . . .

Cummings, T., 'The Sound of Philadelphia', Eyre Methuen, 1975.
Fabian, Frankie Avalon et al., 'From Bobby-sox To Stockings',
   MGM 2315 280.
Hopkins, J., 'The Rock Story', Signet Books, 1970.
Belz, C. 'The Story Of Rock', Harper & Row, 1973.

SHAKIN' ALL OVER

Cochran, Eddie, 'On The Air', United Artists UAS 29380. Cochran
   on Jack Good's TV show 'Boy Meets Girl' shortly before his
   death.
Ellis, Royston, 'The Big Beat Scene', Four Square Books, 1961.
Laing, Dave, 'The Sound Of Our Time', Sheed & Ward, 1970.
Richard, Cliff and Latham, Bill, 'Which One's Cliff?', Hodder &
   Stoughton, 1977.
Wilde, Marty, 'Good Rockin' Then And Now', Philips 6382 102.

ROCK 'N' ROLL IS HERE TO STAY

Curtis, Mac, 'Rockin' Mother', Radar RAD 22.
Smith, Warren, Knox, Buddy, Feathers, Charlie and Scott, Jack,
   'Four Rock 'n' Roll Legends', EMI Harvest SHSM 2024. Recorded
   live in London, April 1977.

British rock 'n' roll bands

Matchbox, 'Setting The Woods On Fire', Chiswick WIK 10.
Various 'Best Of British Rockabilly', Charly CBM 2002.

Whirlwind, 'Blowin' Up A Storm', Chiswick WIK 7.

For the flavour of the late 1950s in Britain see:

Fletcher, Colin, Beat And Gangs on Merseyside, reprinted in
    T. Raison (ed.), 'Youth In New Society', Rupert Hart-Davis,
    1966.
Gosling, Ray, 'Sum Total', Faber & Faber, 1962.
MacInnes, Colin, Sharp Schmutter, in 'England, Half English',
    Penguin, 1966.

GENERAL READING

Hardy, Phil and Laing, Dave (eds.), 'The Encyclopaedia of Rock'
    vol. 1, Panther, 1976.
Jenkinson, Philip and Warner, Alan, 'Celluloid Rock', Lorrimer,
    1974.
Krivine, John, 'Jukebox Saturday Night', New English Library,
    1977. The history of the jukebox.
Melly, George, 'Revolt Into Style', Allen Lane, 1970.
Nite, Norm N., 'Rock On', Popular Library, 1977.
Shaw, Arnold, 'The Rockin' Fifties', Hawthorne, 1974.

Finally, two British magazines devoted to rock 'n' roll: 'Not
Fade Away' (published by the Vintage Rock 'n' Roll Appreciation
Society), and 'New Kommotion' which has no rival in the depth of
its research and the quality of its articles on rock 'n' roll - it is
a fine magazine by any standards. Both are obtainable from Com-
pendium Books, 234 Camden High Street, London, NW1 or from
the following highly recommended record shops which specialise
in rock 'n' roll:

Rock On, 3 Kentish Town Road, London, NW1
Smokey Joe's Cafe, 41 Elm Road, New Malden, Surrey.
Vintage Record Centre Ltd, 91 Roman Way, London, N7 8UN

15 'SOUL AND MOTOWN'
by Simon Frith

BOOKS

It is impossible to understand soul music without understanding the black American experience from which it emerged. The best books about this experience have little to say about music directly but are essential reading none the less.

The best account of black American life just before the rise of soul is a novel:

Ellison, Ralph, 'Invisible Man', Penguin, 1965.

And the seminal statement of the new black consciousness of the early 1960s is:

Baldwin, James, 'The Fire Next Time', Penguin, 1967.

For black city life, of which soul was most clearly the sound, see:

Brown, Claude, 'Manchild in the Promised Land', Penguin, 1969.

This is a wonderful non-fictional account of Harlem and should be read in conjunction with the thrillers of Chester Himes, which use many of the stereotypes that featured in the black films and music of the late 1960s. His best book is

Himes, Chester, 'Cotton Comes to Harlem', Panther, 1966.

The essential black power writings are:

Malcolm X, 'The Autobiography of Malcolm X', Penguin, 1969.
Cleaver, Eldridge, 'Soul on Ice', Delta, 1968.
Jackson, George, 'Soledad Brother', Penguin, 1971.

Books on soul music itself are few and far between, and most of them are, surprisingly, by British authors. The best account of black popular music from the 1950s to the mid-1960s remains:

Gillett, Charlie, 'The Sound of the City', Sphere, 1971.

For a more specialised account of the 1950s black group sound see:

Millar, Bill, 'The Drifters', Studio Vista, 1971.

There is also a splendid book on gospel music:

Heilbut, Tony, 'The Gospel Sound', Anchor, 1975.

For basic facts and figures of the development of soul from the mid-1960s to the mid-1970s see:

Hoare, Ian (ed.), 'The Soul Book', Methuen, 1975.

This is the only comprehensive book on soul and contains also an important essay by Ian Hoare on soul lyrics.
   There is, as yet, no good book on soul's subsequent progress or on the rise of disco, though part of the story is told in:

Cummings, Tony, 'The Sound of Philadelphia', Methuen, 1975.

The best way to keep up with soul is by reading the magazines, 'Black and Soul', and 'Black Music'. The best commentator on disco is Davitt Sigerson, who writes for 'Melody Maker'.

   For interesting and important attempts to relate black music to its American social and cultural setting see:

Haralambos, Michael, 'Right On: From Blues to Soul in Black
   America', Edison Bluesbooks, 1974.
Jones, Leroi, 'Black Music', Morrow, 1967.
Keil, Charles, 'Urban Blues', Chicago University Press, 1966.
Marcus, Greil, 'Mystery Train', Dutton, 1975. See chapter 3.

The most sensitive accounts of individual soul stars are in

Lydon, Michael, 'Rock Folk', Delta, 1973.
Lydon, Michael, 'Boogie Lightning', Dial, 1974.

The only worthwhile soul biography is

Henderson, D., 'Jimi Hendrix', Doubleday, 1979.

RECORDS

The history of soul has been, to a large extent, a history of singles. The greatest soul records have made their immediate mark on charts and dance floors, on the radio and jukeboxes, and then faded into memory. These records remain available, but on anthology LPs, and these LPs are constantly being deleted, repackaged, reissued. This makes it difficult to compile a list of essential records, and it is easier just to offer a rule of thumb: all the essential soul stars, from Ray Charles and Sam Cooke through to the Commodores and Earth Wind and Fire, have Greatest Hits packages available, and these are the best introductions to their work. But for an introduction to soul generally, it is probably better to think in terms of labels rather than artists. As an introduction to the strength and range of soul music, the following albums are indispensable:

   'Atlantic Black Gold', Atlantic.
   'The Motown Story', Tamla Motown boxed set.
   'The Stax Story', vols 1 and 2, Stax.

   The latter two records are also well annotated, and between them these records cover the range of classical 60s' soul music.

As an introduction to the musical roots of soul the best records are:

'This is How it all Began', vols 1 and 2, Specialty.

These two anthologies cover all the bases of pre-soul 1950s' black music blues, doo-wop, gospel, rock'n'roll and pop. Specialty have also issued a fascinating LP comparing the gospel and pop styles of Sam Cooke:

'The Two Sides of Sam Cooke', Specialty.

Soul music and disco in the 1970s is less well represented in general anthologies, but an exhilarating introduction to the new dance sounds can be got from:

'Disco Party', Polydor. A 1974 anthology which ranges from James Brown funk to Gloria Gaynor's New York slickness.
'Saturday Night Fever', RSO, the 1977 anthology which puts the Bee Gees' pop falsettos in the context of the black sounds of the Trammps and Tavares.

Otherwise, a list of recommended soul albums can only be idiosyncratic. The one essential record is, obviously:

'A 25th Anniversary in Show Business Salute to Ray Charles', Atlantic.

The following records were significant as albums (rather than as collections of singles):

Bobby 'Blue' Band, 'Two Steps from the Blues', Duke.
Brown, James, 'Live at the Apollo', Polydor.
Chairman of the Board, 'Skin I'm In', Invictus.
Chic, 'C'est Chic' Atlantic.
The Commodores, 'Zoom', Tamla Motown.
The Commodores, 'Machine Gun', Tamla Motown.
Franklin, Aretha, 'I Never Loved a Man the way I Love You', Atlantic.
Gaye, Marvin, 'What's Goin' On', Tamla Motown.
Gaye, Marvin, 'Let's Get It On', Tamla Motown.
Green, Al, 'I'm still in Love with you', London.
Hayes, Isaac, 'Hot Buttered Soul', Stax.
Hendrix, Jimi, 'Electric Ladyland', Track.
Jackson, Millie, 'Caught Up', Spring.
Mayfield, Curtis, 'Superfly', Curtom.
The O'Jays, 'Ship Ahoy', Philadelphia International.
Parliament, 'Mothership Connection', Casablanca.
Sly and the Family Stone, 'There's a Riot Going On', Epic.
Wonder, Stevie, 'Talking Book', Tamla Motown.
Wonder, Stevie, 'Innervisions', Tamla Motown.

16 'REGGAE AND CARIBBEAN MUSIC'
by Dick Hebdige

RECORDS

The following list is composed entirely of LPs. This is because the distribution network for reggae singles is so uneven and idiosyncratic that there can be no guarantee that the recommended 45s would be available from high-street record stores. The list should thus be read as a loose guideline. But all of the records recommended below are available from Virgin Records which has branches dotted throughout the country. Beyond this, I would suggest that pupils interested in reggae should be encouraged to bring their own collections into school.

Caribbean folk music

This is difficult to get hold of but Ethnic Folkways specialises in the area and has a wide selection of Caribbean folk albums. I would recommend two Folkways albums - 'Steel Band' and 'Bongo, Backra and Coolie' - the last one contains examples of Kumina music. Otherwise try 'Grounation', Ashanti Records, 1974 by Count Ossie and the Mystic Revelations of Rastafari - a 3-LP set of traditional Rastafarian burru drumming and singing. Ras Michael and the Sons of Negus combine burru music with reggae on 'Nyahbinghi' (Trojan, 1974).

Latin American and Cuban music

Again not easy to track down but a certain amount of Latin American traditional folk music is available on labels such as Folkways and Ocora. Urban and commercial music is issued in large quantities, but as availability rapidly changes, readers should consult specialist record shops, such as Sterns, 126 Tottenham Court Road, London W.1.

Calypso

Mighty Sparrow, 'Hotter Than Ever' (Trojan, 1972). Teachers should be cautious here as many of the calypsos included are extremely lewd.
Mighty Sparrow, 'Sparrow Power' (Trojan, 1974). Safer

Reggae compilation albums

There are many excellent compilation albums which bring together accepted 'classics' by a range of established stars:

'The Front Line' Virgin, 1976. Excellent value: contains tracks by, amongst others, The Mighty Diamonds, U. Roy, I-Roy and the Gladiators.

'The Harder They Come', Island, 1974. The soundtrack to the film. Tracks by Jimmy Cliff, Desmond Dekker, The Slickers, Toots and the Maytals and others.

'This Is Reggae Music', Island, 1976. Again good value: includes tracks by Aswad, Prince Jazzbo, Bunny Wailer, Junior Murvin, Max Romeo, Lee Perry and Jah Lion.

'This Is Reggae Music' (double album), Island, 1977. Includes tracks by Zap Pow, the Wailers, Joe Higgs, Jimmy Cliff, Toots and the Maytals, the Heptones, Third World, Justin Hines and the Dominoes, Augustus Pablo and Burning Spear.

'Tighten Up', vols 1-8, Trojan, 1967-72. This series contained many early reggae classics.

Try also:

'One Big Happy Family', Island, 1978.

'Roots, Rock Reggae', Creole, 1978.

'The Sounds of the Islands', Trojan. Useful because it contains tracks by 'mainstream' singers like John Holt and Pluto Shervington.

Ska

Prince Buster, 'Fabulous', Trojan reissue, 1979.

Various artists, 'Intensified: Original Ska 1962-66', Island 1979.

Reggae

Big Youth, 'Dreadlocks Dread', Virgin, 1978.

Burning Spear, 'Dry and Heavy', Island.

Culture, 'Two Sevens Clash', Lightning, 1978.

Bob Marley and the Wailers, 'Catch A Fire', Island, 1972.

Bob Marley and the Wailers, 'Burnin' ', Island, 1973.

Bob Marley and the Wailers, 'Natty Dread', Island, 1974.

Bob Marley and the Wailers, 'Rastaman Vibration', Island, 1975.

Bob Marley and the Wailers, 'Exodus', Island, 1976.

Bob Marley and the Wailers, 'Birth Of A Legend'.

Mighty Diamonds, 'Right Time', Virgin, 1976.

Junior Murvin, 'Police And Thieves', Island, 1976.

Max Romeo, 'War in Babylon, Island, 1976.

I. Roy, 'Crisus Time', Virgin, 1976.

Third World, 'Third World', Island, 1976.

Toots and the Maytals, 'Reggae Got Soul', Island.
Toots and the Maytals, 'Funky Kingston', Island.
Peter Tosh, 'Legalise It', Columbia.
U. Roy, 'Dread in a Babylon', Virgin.
Bunny Wailer, 'Blackheart Man', Island, 1976.
Rico, 'Man From Wareika', Island, 1977.

Dub

This can be a treacherous and difficult area. Generally it's best
to look for the names of the producers and/or the studio musicians
rather than for individual titles. However, I would recommend two
LPs in particular:

The Upsetters, 'Super Ape', Island, 1976.
African Dub, 'Chapter 3', Joe Gibbs Records, 1977.

   The names to look for in dub are Lee Perry, Joe Gibbs, Augustus
Pablo, Linval Thompson. The studio groups are The Upsetters,
the Revolutionaries, the Aggrovators, and Skin, Flesh and Bones.
Also Fat Man Riddim Section.

'Commercial' reggae

John Holt, 'One Thousand Volts of Holt', Trojan.
Johnny Nash, 'Greatest Hits', CBS.

British reggae

Linton Kwesi Johnson (Poet and the Roots), 'Dread Beat and
   Blood', Virgin, 1978.
Linton Kwesi Johnson (Poet and the Roots), 'Forces of Victory',
   Island, 1979.
Steel Pulse, 'Handsworth Revolution', Island, 1978.

BOOKS

Barrett, L.E., 'The Rastafarians: The Dreadlocks Of Jamaica',
   Sangster, 1977.
Davis, Stephen and Simon, Peter, 'Reggae Bloodlines', Anchor,
   1977.
Kallyndyr, Rolston and Dairymple, Henderson, 'Reggae: A People's
   Music', Carib-Arawak, 1976.
Nettleford, Rex, 'Mirror, Mirror - Identity, Race and Protest in
   Jamaica', Collins & Sangster, 1970.
Nettleford, Rex, Smith, M.G. and Augier, R., 'Report On the
   Rastafarian Movement in Kingston, Jamaica', Institute of Social
   and Economic Research, UCWI, Kingston, 1960.

Owens, Joseph, 'Dread - The Rastafarians Of Jamaica', Sangster, 1976.
Patterson, Orlando, 'The Children of Sisyphus', Houghton Mifflin, 1965.
Plummer, J., 'Movement of Jah People', Press Gang, 1979.
Thomas, Michael and Boot, Adrian, 'Babylon on a Thin Wire', Thames & Hudson, 1976.

Marcus Garvey

Cronon, E.D., 'Black Moses', University of Wisconsin Press, 1966.

Black-police relations

Hall, S., Jefferson, T., Clarke, J. and Roberts, B., 'Policing The Crisis', Macmillan, 1978.
Humphrey, Derek and John, Gus, 'Police Power and Black People', Panther, 1972.
Humphrey, Derek and John, Gus, 'Because They're Black', Penguin, 1974.
Smith, David, 'Racial Disadvantage in Britain', Penguin, 1977.

Youth culture

Hall, S., Jefferson, T. and Clarke, J. (eds), 'Resistance Through Rituals', Hutchinson, 1976.
Hebdige, Dick, 'Subculture: The Meaning of Style', Methuen, 1979.

The Teds
Fyvel, T., 'The Insecure Offenders', Chatto & Windus, 1963.

The mods
Herman, Gary, 'The Who', Studio Vista, 1971.

The skinheads
Daniel, S. and McGuire, P., 'The Paint House: Words from an East End Gang', Penguin, 1972.
Fowler, P., 'Skins Rule', from 'Rock File', Gillett, C. (ed.), New English Library, 1972.
Gayle, Carl, 'Reggae: Soul Of Jamaica', from 'The Story of Pop', no. 25, Phoebus Publications.

Hippies
Neville, R., 'Playpower', Paladin, 1971.

Punk
Parker, T. and Burchill, J., 'The Boy Looked at Johnny', Pluto

118 *Further resources*

Press, 1978. See also D. Hebdige (1979), above.

Immigration

Hiro, Philip, 'Black British, White British', Penguin, 1972.

OTHER RESOURCES

Films

'The Harder They Come', directed by Perry Henzel, 1972.
'Dread, Beat and Blood', directed by Franco Rosso (on the poetry
  and music of Linton Johnson), 1979.

Television programmes

'The Rastafarians'. A programme in the Everyman series broad-
  cast in 1977.

Radio programmes

'Reggae: The Beginnings'
'Rastas and Rude Boys'   produced by Vic Lockwood and
'The Sound System'   presented by Dick Hebdige.

These are available on tape from the Open University. They formed
part of course 'DE. 353 Mass Communications and Society'.

Magazines

See any copy of 'Black Echoes', 'Black Music and Jazz Review',
'Sounds', 'New Musical Express'.

17 'CONTEMPORARY FOLK SONG'

by Brian Carroll

BOOKS

Chapter 1

Grigson, G. (ed.), 'The Penguin Book of Ballads', 1977.
Howes, F., 'Folk Music of Britain and Beyond', Methuen, 1969.
Lloyd, A.L. 'Folk Song in England', Paladin, 1975.
Sharp, C., 'English Folk Song: Some Conclusions', Oxford University Press, 1974.

Chapter 2

Laing, D. 'The Sound of Our Times', Sheed & Ward, 1969.
Leach, R. and Palmer, R., 'Folk Music In School', Cambridge University Press, 1978.

Chapter 3

Guthrie, W., 'Born To Win', Macmillan, 1965.
Lomax, J. and Lomax, A. (eds), 'The Leadbelly Legend', Folkways, 1975.
Sharp, C., 'English Folk Songs from the Southern Appalachian Mountains', Oxford University Press, 1917.
Yurchenko, H., 'The Woody Guthrie Story: A Mighty Hard Road', McGraw Hill, 1970.

Chapter 4

Denisoff, R.S., 'Great Day Coming', University of Illinois Press, 1972.
Denisoff, R.S., 'Sing A Song of Social Significance', Bowling Green University Popular Press, 1972.
Silverman, J., 'Folk Blues', Oak, 1968.
Various authors, 'The Story of Pop', Phoebus Publications, 1974.

Chapter 5

Gray, M., 'Song and Dance Man: The Art of Bob Dylan', Sphere, 1973.

Macgregor, C. (ed.) 'Bob Dylan, A Retrospective', Picador, 1975.
Torres, B. (ed.), 'Knocking On Dylan's Door', Dempsey/Cassell, 1975.

Chapter 6

Bleiweiss, R.M. 'Marching To Freedom, The Life of Martin Luther King, Jnr', Mentor, 1970.
Dallas, K., 'Singers of an Empty Day', Kahn & Averill, 1971.
Grossman, L., 'A Social History of Rock Music', David McKay, 1976.
Okun, M., 'Something to Sing About', Macmillan, 1968.
Pollock, B., 'In Their Own Hands', Collier, 1975.

Chapter 7

Belz, C., 'The Story of Rock', Oxford University Press, 1972.
Mabey, R., 'The Pop Process', Hutchinson Educational, 1969.
Mabey, R., 'Anatomy of Pop', BBC Publications, 1977.
Marcus, G.(ed), 'Rock 'n' Roll Will Stand', Beacon Press, 1969.
Rodnitzky, J., 'Minstrels of the Dawn: The Folk Protest Singer as a Cultural Hero', Nelson Hall, 1976.
Shaw, A., 'The Rock Revolution', Collier Macmillan, 1969.
Torres, B. (ed.), 'The Rolling Stone Reader', vol. 2, Bantam, 1974.

Chapter 8

Sarlin, B., 'Turn it Up (I Can't Hear the Words)', Coronet Books, 1975.

General

Shaljean, B., (ed.), 'Folk Directory', English Folk, 1978.
Stambler, I. (ed.), 'The Encyclopaedia of Pop, Rock and Soul', St James Press, 1975.
Stambler, I. and Landon, G. (eds), 'The Encyclopaedia of Folk, Country and Western', St James Press, 1975.

PERIODICALS

'Folk News', monthly (ed. K. Dallas).
'Folk Review', monthly (ed. F. Woods).
'Melody Maker', weekly (two pages on folk).
'Sing Out', monthly (imported, usually only available at folk record shops).

RECORDS

The following records are listed in the order in which discussion
of the artists concerned appears in the book.

Leadbelly, 'Take This Hammer', Folkways, FTS 31019.
Guthrie, Woody, 'Dust Bowl Ballads', Folkways, FH5212.
Guthrie, Woody, 'Woody Guthrie Sings Folk Songs', Folkways,
    FA 2483. (Features Woody with Leadbelly, Cisco Houston and
    Sonny Terry.)
Seeger, Pete, 'Broadside Ballads', Folkways, FH 5302.
Seeger, Pete, 'The Best of Pete Seeger', CBS, 68201. Double
    album.
Peter, Paul and Mary, 'In Concert', vol. 1, Warner Brothers,
    WS 8158.
Dylan, Bob, 'The Freewheelin' Bob Dylan', CBS, BPG 62193.
Dylan, Bob, 'Bringing It All Back Home', CBS, 62515.
Baez, Joan, 'Come From The Shadows', A & M, AMLH 64339.
Baez, Joan, 'Gulf Winds', A & M, AMLH 64603.
Paxton, Tom, 'Ramblin' Boy', Elektra, EKL 7277.
Ochs, Phil, 'Chords of Fame', A & M, AMIM 64599. Double Album.
Sainte-Marie, Buffy, 'It's My Way', Fontana, TFL 6040.
Collins, Judy, 'Wildflowers', Elektra, EKS 74012.
Dylan, Bob, 'Blonde On Blonde', CBS, CBZ 66012. Double Album.
Dylan, Bob, 'Blood On The Tracks', CBS, CBS69097.
Mitchell, Joni, 'Clouds', Reprise, K44070.
Jansch, Bert and Renbourn, John, 'Bert and John', Transatlantic,
    TRA 144.
The Pentangle, 'Sweet Child', Transatlantic, TRA 178. Double
    album.
Donovan, 'Barabajagal', Epic, XSB 150537.
The Incredible String Band, 'The Hangman's Beautiful Daughter',
    Elektra, K42002.
Fairport Convention, 'What We Did On Our Holidays', Island,
    1LPS 9092.
Fairport Convention, 'Tipplers' Tales', Vertigo, 9102022.
Steeleye Span, 'Please To See The King', Mooncrest, CREST 8.
Steeleye Span, 'Storm Force Ten', Crysalis, CHR 1151.
Thompson, Richard and Thompson, Linda, 'I Want To See The
    Bright Lights Tonight', Island, 1LPS 9266.
Carthy, Martin and Swarbrick, Dave, 'Byker Hill', Topic, 12TS342.

Folkways records are imported from America. They can be
obtained through shops specialising in folk music, such as Collets,
180 Shaftesbury Avenue, London WC2.
    There is a useful three-album set of American traditional songs,
called 'Anthology of American Folk Music', issued by Folkways
vol. 1, 'Ballads', FA 2951; vol. 2, 'Social Music', FA 2952; vol. 3,
'Songs', FA 2953.
    Similarly, there are two three-album sets, issued by The Library
of Congress, of the recordings made by John and Alan Lomax of

the songs of Leadbelly, Elektra, EKL 301/2; and of Woody
Guthrie, Elektra, EKL 271/2.

18 'ROCK MUSIC'
by Dave Rogers

THE EARLY 1960s

Cliff Richard: '40 Golden Greats', (EMI EMTV 6); Billy Fury:
'The Golden Years of Billy Fury' (K-Tel NE 1030); Joe Meek's
production can be found on 'The Joe Meek Story' (Decca DPA
3035/6) and on a recently released John Leyton EP (EMI 2699);
Sam Cooke: 'The Golden Age Of Sam Cooke' (RCA RS 1054); Ray
Charles: 'Salute To Ray Charles' (Polydor 2659 009); Everly
Brothers: 'Walk Right Back With The Everly Bros.' (Warner K.
56168); Brenda Lee: 'The Brenda Lee Story' (MCA MCDW 428);
Roy Orbison: 'Greatest Hits', (CBS MNT 64663); Bobby Vee:
'Legendary Masters Series' (United Artists UAD 60055/6).

THROUGH MERSEYBEAT AND THE R'N'B CLUBS TO
MID-1960s POP

Chris May and Tim Phillips: 'British Beat' (Sociopack Publications,
1974); Bill Harry: 'Merseybeat: The Beginnings Of The Beatles'
(Omnibus, 1977) (selected issues of Liverpool's local music paper
of the early 1960s reprinted and collected together).
   Mods and rockers: S. Cohen: 'Folk Devils and Moral Panics'
(Paladin, 1973); Gary Herman: 'The Who' (Studio Vista 1971);
Tom Wolfe: The Noonday Underground, in 'The Pump House Gang'
(Bantam, 1969: and, more generally, Peter Laurie: 'Teenage
Revolution' (Anthony Blond, 1965).
   'Hits Of The Mersey Era' (EMI NUT 1); 'The Beat Merchants
1963-64' (United Artists UDM 101/2); 'The Sixties File' (Pye FILD
006-1/2); 'Blues Roots: British R'n'B' (Decca ROOTS 6);
   Georgie Fame and The Blue Flames: 'R'n'B At The Flamingo'
(Columbia SX 1599); Spencer Davis Group: 'The Best Of Spencer
Davis' (Island ILPS 9070); Yardbirds: 'Five Live Yardbirds'
(Columbia SX 1677); Manfred Mann: 'The Best Of Manfred Mann'
(EMI NUT 7); Kinks: 'The Kinks File' (Pye FILD 001); 'Intensified!
Original Ska 1962-66' (Island IRSP 2).

BY THIS TIME, IN THE UNITED STATES

Joan Baez: 'The Joan Baez File' (Pye FILD 010); Phil Ochs:
'Chords Of Fame' (A & M AMLM 64599); Lovin' Spoonful: 'The
Lovin' Spoonful File' (Pye FILD 009).

123

The impact of the Beatles in the US ('The Beatles At The Holly-
wood Bowl', EMI EMTV 4) can be seen in 'Nuggets' (Elektra K
62012).
    For Bob Dylan see Anthony Scaduto: 'Bob Dylan' (Abacus,
1973); Michael Gray: 'Song And Dance Man: The Art Of Bob Dylan'
(Sphere, 1973); and for folk and folk-rock see section by Brian
Carroll.
    Buffalo Springfield: 'Retrospective' (Atlantic K 40071); Doors:
'Weird Scenes Inside The Goldmine' (Elektra K 62009); Steve
Miller Band: 'Sailor' (Capital ST 2984); Quicksilver Messenger
Service: 'Happy Trails' (Capitol EST 120); Love: 'Forever
Changes' (Elektra K 42015); Bob Dylan and The Band: 'The Base-
ment Tapes' (CBS 88147); MC5: 'Kick Out The Jams' (Atlantic
K 42027).

Books

(Greil Marcus (ed.): 'Rock and Roll Will Stand' (Beacon Press,
1969); R. Burt and P. North: 'West Coast Story' (Phoebus, 1977);
D. Landau: 'Janis Joplin: Her Life And Times' (Paperback Library,
1971); John Sinclair: 'Guitar Army' (Douglas Book Corporation,
1972).

BACK TO BRITAIN AND ON TO THE END OF THE 1960s

Performers

Rick Sanders: 'Pink Floyd' (Futura, 1976); Steve Turner: 'Conver-
sation With Eric Clapton' (Sphere, 1976); and Chris Welch:
'Hendrix' (Ocean Books, 1972).

General

Richard Neville: 'Playpower' (Palladin, 1971); Richard Mabey:
'The Pop Process' (Hutchinson, 1969).
    Beatles: 'Beatles 1967-70' (Parlophone PCS 7027); Cream: 'Best
Of Cream' (Polydor 583 060); John Mayall's Bluesbreakers: 'Blues
Breakers' (Decca 4804); Fleetwood Mac: 'Vintage Years' (CBS
88227); Chicken Shack: 'Forty Blue Fingers' (Blue Horizon
7-63203); Eric Clapton: 'History Of Eric Clapton' (Polydor 2659
012); Soft Machine: 'Volumes One and Two' (Probe GTSP 204);
The Move: 'Shazam/Move' (Pye/Cube TOOFA 1/2); Monkees:
'Monkees' (EMI SPR 90032); Hollies: '20 Golden Greats' (EMI EMTV
11);

Live music

Rolling Stones: 'Get Your Ya Yas Out' (Decca SKL 5065); Janis
Joplin with Big Brother And The Holding Company: 'Cheap
Thrills' (CBS 63392); and various artists: 'Woodstock' (Atlantic
K 60001).

AND INTO THE 1970s - NEW DIRECTIONS, OLD WAYS,
LOOSE ENDS AND PRODUCT

Neil Young: 'After The Goldrush' (Reprise K44088); Jackson
Browne: 'Late For The Sky' (Asylum K43007); Allman Brothers:
'Live At The Fillmore East' (Capricorn 2659 039); Eagles: 'Their
Greatest Hits' (Asylum K53017); Lou Reed: 'Rock 'n' Roll Animal'
(RCA APLI 0472); Alice Cooper: 'School's Out' (Warner K56007);
Blue Oyster Cult: 'Agents Of Fortune' (CBS 81385); Boston:
'Boston' (Epic EPC 81611); The Osmonds: 'Our Best To You' (MGM
2315 300).

WHILE IN BRITAIN

Slade: 'Sladest' (Polydor 2442 119); Sweet: 'The Golden Greats'
   (RCA PL 25111); Black Sabbath: 'Greatest Hits' (NEMS NEL
6009); Status Quo: 'Blue For You' (Vertigo 9102 006).

Books

I. Hoare, C. Anderson, T. Cummings and S. Frith: 'The Soul
Book' (Eyre Methuen, 1975); T. Cummings: 'The Sound Of Phila-
delphia' (Eyre Methuen, 1975); R. Sarlin: 'Turn It Up (I Can't
Hear The Words)' (Coronet, 1975); J. Pidgeon: 'Rod Stewart And
The Changing Faces' (Panther, 1976); and I. Hunter: 'Diary Of
A Rock 'n' Roll Star' (Panther, 1974).

EARLY 1970s RESURGENCE

David Bowie: 'Aladdin Sane' (RCA RS1001) and 'Heroes' (RCA PL
12522); John Lennon: 'Imagine' (Parlophone PAS 10004); Roxy
Music: 'Greatest Hits' (Polydor 2302 073); Rolling Stones: 'Exile
On Main Street' (Rolling Stones COC 59100); Who: 'Who's Next'
(Track 2408 102), and 'Quadrophenia' (Track 2657 013); Bob
Marley and The Wailers: 'Live!' (Island ILPS 9376); New York
Dolls: 'New York Dolls' (Mercury 6641 631); Iggy And The Stooges:
'Raw Power' (CBS 31464); Steely Dan: 'Greatest Hits' (ABC ABCD
616).

Books

R. Greenfield: 'A Journey Through America With The Rolling
Stones' (Panther, 1975); G. Tremlett: 'The David Bowie Story'
(Futura, 1975); N. Schaffner: 'The Beatles Forever' (McGraw-
Hill, 1978); C. McKnight and J. Tobler: 'Bob Marley – The Roots
of Reggae' (Star Books, 1977); and J. Plummer: 'Movement of Jah
People' (Press Gang, 1979).

THE MID-1970s: OUT OF THE DEPTHS AND INTO THE FUTURE

Bruce Springsteen: 'Born To Run' (CBS 69170); Brinsley Schwarz:
'15 Thoughts Of Brinsley Schwarz' (United Artists UAK 30177);
Ramones: 'Ramones' (Sire SR 6020); Dr Feelgood: 'Stupidity'
(United Artists UAS 29990); Graham Parker and The Rumour:
'Heat Treatment' (Vertigo 6360 137); Patti Smith: 'Horses' (Arista
ARTY 122); Television: 'Marquee Moon' (Elektra K52046).

THE LATE 1970s PUNK AND THE NEW WAVE

Buzzcocks: 'Another Music In A Different Kitchen' (United Artists
UAG 30159); Jam: 'All Mod Cons' (Polydor POLD 5008); Boomtown
Rats: 'A Tonic For The Troops' (Ensign ENVY 3); Sham 69: 'Tell
Us The Truth' (Polydor 2683 491); Stiff Little Fingers: 'Inflam-
mable Material' (Rough Trade ROUGH 1); Tom Robinson Band:
'Power In The Darkness' (EMI EMC 3226); Siouxsie and The
Banshees: 'The Scream' (Polydor POLD 5009); X-Ray Spex: 'Germ
Free Adolescents' (EMI INS 3023); Penetration: 'Moving Targets'
(Virgin V2109).

Books

R. Stevenson (ed.): 'Sex Pistols File' (Omnibus Press, 1978); F.
and J. Vermorel: 'The Sex Pistols' (Universal Books, 1978); M.
Perry (ed.): 'The Bible' (Omnibus Press, 1978); and J. Burchill
and T. Parsons: 'The Boy Looked At Johnny' (Pluto Press, 1978).
   More generally: for the underground press see R. Lewis: 'Out-
laws Of America' (Penguin, 1972), and for its political preoccupations and involvements see P. Stansill and D.Z. Mairowitz:
'Bamn – Outlaw Manifestos and Ephemera 1965-70' (Penguin, 1971).

Sociology
S. Frith: 'The Sociology Of Rock', (Constable, 1978); S. Hall and
T. Jefferson (eds): 'Resistance Through Rituals – Youth Sub-
cultures In Post-war Britain', (Hutchinson, 1976); D. Hebdige:
'Subculture: The Meaning of Style' (Methuen, 1979). Rock music
in film is covered by P. Jenkinson and A. Warner in 'Celluloid
Rock' (Lorrimer, 1974).

Background to the music business
M. Wale: 'Vox Pop' (Harrap, 1972); Derek Taylor: 'As Time Goes
By' (Sphere, 1974). Jeff Nuttall: 'Bomb Culture' (Paladin, 1970)
is a personal but highly recommended view of pop culture and
political involvement in the post-war period. 'The Rolling Stone
Interviews', vols 1 and 2 (Warner, 1971 and 1973): B. Fong-
Torres (ed.): 'The Rolling Stone Rock 'n' Roll Reader' (Bantam,
1974); P. Hardy and D. Laing (eds): 'The Encyclopaedia of Rock',
vols 2 and 3 (Panther, 1976; packaged in one edition with vol. 1
by Aquarius Books, 1977), N. Logan and B. Woffinden: 'The
Illustrated New Musical Express Encyclopaedia of Rock' (Salamander
Books, 1977). C. Gillett and S. Frith (eds): 'Rock File', vols 2,
3, 4 and 5 (Panther, 1970); J. and T. Rice, P. Gambaccini, M.
Read: 'The Guinness Book of British Hit Singles' (Guinness
Superlatives, 1979).